# What some audiences said after John-Paul Flintoff followed the guidance provided in this book

*"To tell you the truth, I only went to see this guy to get the afternoon off work... So I was really surprised that I enjoyed it."*

Attendee, in-person event

*"I did enjoy listening. The best thing was that he didn't just keep going on about himself, like one or two that had come earlier that week."*

Attendee, in-person event

*"There are few occasions when you can genuinely forget that you are 'inside' when you are a guest of Her Majesty, but this was surely one of them, and it lasted for a whole afternoon."*

Attendee, in-person event at HMP Dumfries

*"One of the most powerful talks that I have ever been to. It was so raw, honest and exceptionally brave."*

Attendee, illustrated talk online

*"I was the one at the back, sobbing and snotting."*

Attendee, in-person talk, Mishcon de Reya

# A modest book about how to make an adequate speech

John-Paul Flintoff

Published in 2021 by Short Books,
an imprint of Octopus Publishing Group Ltd
Carmelite House
50 Victoria Embankment
London, EC4Y 0DZ
www.octopusbooks.co.uk

An Hachette UK Company
www.hachette.co.uk

10 9 8 7 6 5 4 3

A CIP catalogue record for this book is
available from the British Library.

ISBN: 978-1-78072-603-8

Cover design by Andrew Smith
Interior illustrations by John-Paul Flintoff

Printed and bound in Great Britain by
Clays Ltd, Elcograf S.p.A.

This FSC® label means that materials used for the product
have been responsibly sourced

MIX
Paper from
responsible sources
FSC® C104740

*To Nancy: May you always speak well.*

*A.M.D.G.*

"Churchill's oratory became a remarkably well-tuned and well-practised political instrument. Indeed, considering that he never built up a regional power base in the country or a personal following at Westminster, that he changed his party allegiance twice, that his judgement was often faulty, that his administrative talents were uneven, and that his understanding of ordinary people was minimal, it is arguable that oratory was Churchill's only real instrument…"

David Cannadine, *The Great Speeches*

"He almost did not come to that meeting. He was tired; the weather was bad, he hoped not many would show up… His speech lasted almost an hour."

Garry Wills, *Martin Luther King is Still on the Case*

"It is better to die on your feet then to live on your knees."

Dolores Ibarruri, known as "La Pasionaria"

# CONTENTS

The backstory * Why only adequate? * Functions
of oratory * The author's credentials * Reasons you
shouldn't speak * Nobody is beyond help * Necessary
work * Compare and contrast * The five parts
of oratory

The six key questions * Who are you talking to? * What
do you intend to talk about? * Why are you talking
about it? * Where, and When? * How? * Free speech,
really? * Don't be a coward * Writing an outline

People get bored * Take it apart, to see the workings
* The locust years * Reading the room: remember
the Who * Call to action * Unanswered questions *
Dance of the seven veils * Cliffhangers, or loose
ends * A short history of preaching in Western Europe
* Secular inductive sermons * Fresh and honest *
You aren't eight years old * Play with the structure *
Something confessional * On going blank * Torture
the hero * What happened in Mexico

# INTRODUCTION

*We often forgive those who bore us, but we cannot forgive those who find us boring.*

La Rochefoucauld

## The backstory

Which of these situations is most like your own?

A young woman, talking to her mother in the kitchen, is surprised to find herself say she wants to make her first public speech.

A retired bank manager in Yorkshire wakes up one morning and remembers he must give an amusing after-dinner speech down south.

A pair of young men sit down to write an entertaining routine for their sister's wedding.

A woman living in Norway reads a book about changing the world and decides she must somehow get the author to speak in her native Greece.

An Englishman at a conference in Mexico panics as he

realises that the speakers before him have already covered his best material.

A washed-up politician writes a speech intended to convince his party leaders to change direction dramatically and at once.

A woman offers to give the "father of the bride" speech at the wedding of a friend who is estranged from her father.

An author of thirteen books contemplates, with dread, the prospect of his first online book launch, on camera, with a paying audience he won't be able to see.

In China, a preacher-in-training reads the book of Isaiah and sketches ideas for turning it into a sermon.

These are some of the people whose triumphs and disasters you will read about in this book.

But let's begin with the Englishman in Mexico...

A few years ago, I was invited to speak at a conference there. It would turn out to be a memorable event, but not for reasons I'd have chosen.

I'd never heard of this conference, but it was obviously quite a big deal, because the person who invited me was just one relatively small part of a larger team. I was to talk to so-and-so about travel arrangements, and whatsername about my fee.

To be perfectly clear, I was excited to be asked. For most of my career I'd done little public speaking, and I was enjoying it as a newish experience. By then, I'd given quite a few talks, in a number of countries. Mostly in London, but also a little around Europe and even in Asia and North America. It was not always a big deal, and I not uncommonly found myself facing a smallish audience, but I relished turning up to talk to people about the things I care about.

I want to make that perfectly clear, because I know some people absolutely dread public speaking. And those people may include you.

I understand the dread of public speaking, because I've felt that way myself in the past. But at this particular time, I enjoyed it. And people told me I was good at it – sometimes very good – with a couple of painful exceptions, which I'll come back to.

So I went to Mexico.

On the plane, for eleven hours or so, I attempted to teach myself Spanish using an audio download. I would be delivering my talk in English, with simultaneous translation into Spanish through the earpieces supplied to every member of the audience, but I thought it would be polite, and more friendly, to start with a spot of their native language.

In Mexico City, coming out of customs, I was greeted by a man in a smart shirt and blazer, holding up a sign with my name on it. This wasn't any old sign – not the usual laminated sheet of paper, or portable whiteboard with hastily scribbled handwriting. This sign was shaped like a massive table-tennis bat, and my name had been printed onto it in full colour.

The man called me Sir, and insisted on carrying my bag.

Again, that wasn't entirely unusual in the circumstances, but something in his manner gave me the impression that he felt astonishingly privileged to meet me. It was around this point that I started wondering if I had been invited by mistake. They thought I was someone else!

Of course, I didn't spoil the driver's pleasure by saying

anything like that out loud. After all, I was in Mexico now. The organisers had spent all that money on my ticket, and my hotel, and I would jolly well have to give the best talk I could manage. Thank goodness I'd practised Spanish: I'd be able to apologise in my hosts' own language if their embarrassing mistake about my identity became apparent.

(See how high I was aiming! See what confidence I had in myself!)

The city where I was speaking was several hours' drive from the capital, and the young man with the large table-tennis bat led me to a minibus. A group of people who looked like academics, with untidy clothes and spectacles, and whitish hair, stood chatting together in North American accents. (And, as it turned out, they were academics.) When the time came to climb aboard, I stepped back to allow them inside first. As a result, I found myself sitting apart, and for most of the journey they talked among themselves. Which was fine by me: many hours had passed since I woke in London, and I'd been working hard at my Spanish on the plane; once we had cleared the dreadful rush-hour traffic in Mexico City, the rocking of the minibus sent me to sleep.

Every so often, I woke and caught short passages of conversation between my fellow passengers. I had the impression they all knew each other. They seemed to meet regularly at conferences all over the Americas. They'd evidently spoken at this conference before now, and spoke of the man in charge by his first name, like an old friend.

I had never met him, or spoken with him, and wouldn't actually do so until I was on stage, mic in hand.

Perhaps noticing that I had woken, one of the women

asked me about myself. When I started to answer, my own British accent startled me. I was feeling more and more like an outsider.

An imposter.

Sound familiar?

At the hotel, I was checked into a luxurious suite, where I slept soundly and woke the next morning in time for a splendid breakfast, before being collected in a new minibus and driven to the vast conference venue. I wasn't talking till the next day, but having nothing better to do – and having been told I should not walk outside the hotel on my own lest I be kidnapped – I decided to pop along and see the venue for myself.

Hurtling down the great boulevards in the minibus, I noticed with the detached interest of a would-be connoisseur that the graffiti looked distinctively Mexican, as if it had been spray-painted by Aztecs: a reminder that I was not in Spain, where I usually practise my lisping Spanish, but in another country altogether.

Climbing out of the vehicle, we were directed towards the green room, and immediately assaulted by the tremendous noise and wind created by a helicopter, from which several people with earpieces leapt as soon as it hit the ground: security people. They were followed by somebody I didn't recognise, but who carried himself with an air of self-importance.

Not for the first time that day, I wondered what I was doing there.

The green room was in fact a large hall (not green), with private spaces along the side for guests, whose names were on the doors, and a space in the middle for us to sit and talk together.

Finding no room with my name on it, I experienced a remarkable transformation: from feeling like an imposter I transitioned instantly to hurt pride. I was outraged to have been overlooked. But a moment's reflection helped me to see that the rooms had been allocated to people speaking today, and my own talk was not until the next day.

Phew.

Indignation melted away. I went to look at the list of speakers – to see if there was anybody I knew.

It was quite a shock to find myself listed among people I have admired for years. There were some names I didn't know, but an awful lot of them were extremely famous. Not just famous in my line of work but famous-famous.

Oh, God.

I decided to go and look at the stage from the audience.

To do this, I had to walk through the backstage area where upcoming speakers waited to go on.

The ones who were going up next wore headsets, with wires running under their clothes and radio transmitters clipped behind them. They stood before a large screen, watching the speaker who was currently on stage, stretching their fingers as if preparing for a swim, or drawing folded papers from their pockets to check their notes (again).

I didn't recognise any of these individuals, but I did recognise their behaviour: they looked extremely nervous.

Quietly stepping down into the auditorium, I came to see why they might feel that way. It was frighteningly big. I guessed there must be about 5,000 people there. Turning to the stage, I watched the current speaker finish, and walk off. He had quite a distance to cover, but mercifully the audience applauded him all the way.

Must have been some talk.

I stayed for a couple of hours, standing in the aisle to watch the audience watch the speakers, one after another.

Gradually, it became clear that all the things I usually talked about were being covered by the speakers before me. Sure, I could use slightly different examples to illustrate my points, but I doubted that my stories, drawn from my life in faraway London, could be more compelling than those the audience had heard already.

What could I possibly add?

At lunchtime, I returned to the green room/hall, and joined a group of other speakers preparing to be taken to a restaurant where we would eat together. They included an American writer I have read avidly for more than a decade; another American, a woman, whose life-story was turned into several series of TV box-set entertainment; and a third American writing superstar whose internationally best-selling memoir was turned into a film starring Hollywood's most highly paid female actor.

And these were just the individuals standing nearest to me.

Others, undoubtedly as famous – and justly so, I'm sure – added to our numbers as we walked outside and across the conference site.

I found myself talking to the husband of the woman whose life-story became a TV box-set. I'd watched it myself, with some enthusiasm, and felt as if I knew him already because he featured as a character, though played by somebody else, a well-known actor.

As before, I kept to myself all thoughts of being an imposter. I didn't cringe, suck up to people, or talk openly about my unworthiness of being among them. As much as it was in my power, I acted as though I belonged there, just like everyone else. After all, that was my face up there, high above the crowd, blown up to vastly bigger than life size, beside that of a great German movie director.

Oh, God.

As we walked, ticket holders spilling out of the auditorium towards us beamed with delight: they hadn't expected to be so close to all these famous speakers during the lunch break. We smiled back, and kept walking. But then I stopped.

I will never know exactly what possessed me to do what I did next. But I can tell you this: I wouldn't have done it if I had known what was going to happen – not even if I'd known that it would work in my favour, eventually, and might even be seen as a blessing.

It would take more than a year to come to terms with it: to be willing to share it with people who weren't there at the time. But with hindsight, I can see that it did help me to become a better public speaker. Certainly a more confident one, more willing to face the danger of it "all going wrong", whatever that might mean.

At any rate, it confirmed ideas that were already settling in my mind about the whole point of addressing an audience, large or small, and about the spirit in which we might do that.

It taught me to be ready for an audience to respond in ways I couldn't expect.

To like my audience, rather than fear it.

To trust myself to say what needs to be said, even (or especially) things I might prefer to keep hidden.

To make use of my body, not just my brain.

And to tailor what I say to the people in front of me, rather than repeat, hollowly, exactly what I have said to others elsewhere, perhaps many times before. It's just a lot more fun that way. And believe it or not, it's easier.

But that didn't come all at once. It would be another 24 hours before I went on stage to deliver my talk. And for much of that time I felt sick. I would have to think again, from first principles, what I was here for.

Many people would do anything to avoid speaking in public. And you can see why: for most of human history, if you had that many eyes on you it meant you were about to be gobbled up.

Only the most important people – kings, emperors, sultans – learned to be comfortable in the gaze of a large public. Most others probably never experienced it – not once, in a whole lifetime – let alone became comfortable with it.

But opportunities to be observed, and listened to, have quickly multiplied. And with these opportunities have come challenges.

As we travel more, so audiences and speakers become more diverse. In fact, even without travel, technology allows us to appear anywhere, and the sudden, mass adoption of online conferencing by people all over the world during the 2020 Covid-19 pandemic rapidly made that an everyday reality.

Consequently, audiences today may be confronted by speakers whose manner, accent and stories baffle them.

Social changes mean that people who previously were deprived of a hearing because of their gender, race or age can now be given a platform (I won't presume to say "enjoy", because they might dread it as much as the next person).

And with every opportunity to speak comes a heavy burden of anxiety:

- Will anybody want to hear this?
- What can I say that hasn't been said already?
- Does my audience hate people like me, for some reason?
- How do I avoid saying something offensive?
- What if people walk out?
- Or fall asleep?
- What if I forget what I was going to say?
- Or overrun the time I've been given, and get hauled off?
- Is it OK to read notes?
- What if somebody asks me a question I don't know the answer to?
- If I tell the truth, will I be sacked?

And so on. I'm sure that if you take a moment to think about it, you can add more scenarios.

This book attempts to address those questions. But it doesn't have the usual motive of setting out to turn you into a big-shot corporate superhero.

There are plenty of books about public speaking that do that. They can be found in any airport bookshop, tempting morsels for business travellers. This book is different. Its modest ambition is to help you become merely adequate at public speaking.

To become adequate, you will overcome the very same difficulties that lie in the way of your becoming actually rather good at it – indeed, you may find that you have overcome them already. And with a spot of luck, "rather good" is what you will turn out to be.

But I'm not making any promises. Because if I do that, I start to feel like a fake. A charlatan.

## Why only "adequate"?

One day in 1815, after watching an accomplished group of Indian jugglers, the English writer William Hazlitt wrote about the experience, commenting that their technical skill seemed to outshine his own.

"The Indian juggler can keep up four brass balls at the same time, which none of us could do to save our lives... Is it a trifling power we see at work, or something next to miraculous?"

Hearing a speech in parliament, Hazlitt continued, did not shake his good opinion of himself. But seeing the Indian jugglers did. "It makes me ashamed. I ask, what is there that I can do as well as this? Nothing. What have I been doing all my life?"

The best he could do was write a description of what the juggler can do. "I have always had this feeling of the inefficacy and slow progress of intellectual compared to mechanical excellence." With juggling, as with other circus tricks, the object to be attained is not a matter of taste or opinion but of actual experiment: if a man is learning to dance on a rope, and isn't careful, Hazlitt says, he will break his neck. "Danger is a good teacher, and makes apt scholars. So are disgrace, defeat, exposure to immediate scorn and laughter. There is no opportunity in such cases for self-delusion – whereas I can make a very bad antithesis in my writing without cutting my fingers."

What this tells us is that writing, unlike juggling, cannot be done to perfection. The same applies to speaking and presenting. Which, if you think about it, should really come as a relief.

If speaking and writing were like maths, we could state propositions with certainty, and even draw graphs to prove them, like this one showing that the ideal speaker stands exactly halfway between pleasing self and pleasing the audience:

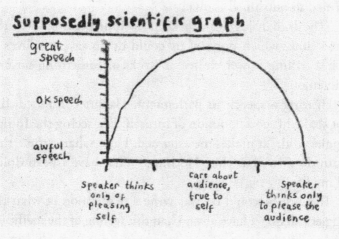

**Supposedly scientific graph**

great speech
OK speech
awful speech

Speaker thinks only of pleasing self
care about audience, true to self
Speaker thinks only to please the audience

But communication is not maths. There are too many variables. People who teach this kind of thing will quote studies showing overwhelming statistical evidence in favour of specific practices and approaches – the right clothing, posture or enunciation. But these are matters of opinion, and even if 99.99% of global audiences have a particular preference, you may find yourself addressing the 0.01%.

What's more, you may simply be unable to meet all the preferences shown by studies, which are liable to include stereotypes. If your audience has a dislike of British people, and you're British, you'll have to do your best to satisfy, despite this awkward fact.

For this reason, it's a good idea to give yourself some options; to learn a little about the sheer variety of factors that affect the conveyance of information, ideas and inspiration from one person to another; to consider briefly the functions of oratory, a little of its history, where ideas come from, and the five steps that teachers of oratory have followed for 20 centuries.

There are two alternatives to doing this prep: burying your head in the sand, and pulling a sickie when the time comes, or trusting your intuition.

The advertising man David Ogilvy, in his amusingly self-promoting manual *Ogilvy on Advertising*, wrote about the lack of ambition he found in many copywriters. "'Raise your sights!' I exhort them. 'Blaze new trails. Hit the ball out of the park!! Compete with the immortals!!!'"

He asked one of these indifferent copywriters what books he had read about advertising. The man told Ogilvy that he had not read any. He preferred to rely on his intuition.

"Suppose your gall-bladder has to be removed this evening," Ogilvy replied. "Will you choose a surgeon who has read some books on anatomy and knows where to find your gall-bladder, or a surgeon who relies on his intuition?"

## Functions of oratory

Students of oratory tend to have two basic motivations: generous, and selfish.

When generosity is the motive, a speaker looks to inform (tell people things they don't know), persuade (help them rethink what they do know), and inspire (encourage them not only to think differently but to do something as a result of that).

Selfishness distorts those motives. Most of us have had the unpleasant experience of listening to someone who appears only to enjoy the sound of their own voice, waste our time and manipulate us for some purpose of their own.

When I was first asked to write this book, I felt a bit sick. You see, I really believe I have valuable ideas to share about this topic, and love to help people tell their stories. I do it a lot. But at the same time, I recognise that others are better qualified. They're better at public speaking, and better at teaching.

And yet... I also don't think anybody in the whole world would be a better choice than me. Because only I can be me. Only I can share what I have to say. So nobody is better than me, and I'm no better than anybody else, either.

What I love most about speaking to an audience is the feeling of connection that comes from talking honestly and

– KAPOW! – seeing people's eyes light up. That comes if I make a joke, but it also comes if I share something painful. KAPOW! Same when I'm listening to other speakers. Only that person can do it, and only to this audience, in this moment. Nobody else can say it. And that individual speaker can't say exactly the same thing to another audience without starting to become a robot. Might as well record a video and never say it again. It has to be fresh.

For related reasons, I'm not particularly interested in mere technique. In themselves, techniques are neither good nor bad – or, rather, they can be both. Hitler was a master of various techniques. But would you buy a book called "How To Speak Like Hitler"? (If you answered "yes", this may not be the book for you.) Of course, the books that are sold in airport bookshops have more appealing titles than that. But after flicking through some of them, I have come to the conclusion they might just as well have that title, because they're all about conquering the world. If not like Hitler, then through the mastery of body-language, timing, rhetoric and generally being a smoothy-chops. I hate that. Pass the sick-bag!

Even the books dressed up to look easy-going promise, too often, that you can learn to get the better of your audience if only you do it the right way. Well, this book is designed for people whose talks may be a bit wonky, no matter how often they practise. People who, despite having peculiar accents, using phrases and idioms weirdly and talking too quietly or too fast, are passionately devoted to sharing ideas that may never have crossed the mind of their audience, and stories about lives that others could never have imagined.

It's for people who long ago rubbed down their wonky bits, hid their natural accent and learned to pace themselves just so – only to find they've lost themselves entirely behind a mask of blandness.

It's for people who have no desire to "own the room", not least because the rapid, widespread shift to online presentations means there's no room to own, and requires speakers more than ever to harness the wisdom and goodwill of participants.

It's for people who aren't out to please (or offend) but to tell it like it is – to say what they need to say, and what the audience needs to hear, in that blessed moment of time when they come together to speak and be heard.

## The author's credentials

The first time I appeared in front of an audience I was seven years old. My father had founded a Shakespeare festival in Brussels, where we lived and he worked. He cast me as Moth, the pageboy in *Love's Labour's Lost*. Mum made my pageboy outfit. All I had to do was walk on stage at the front of a group of four men, who wanted to get to know the four women already onstage. I had to make a little speech acknowledging the women's beauty and talking up the men a bit. Nothing too complicated.

I had my lines by heart and I was ready to go. The four men (including my father) lined up behind me. I walked on, holding my head high as instructed. I said my speech perfectly, but felt terribly confused because the audience laughed. I wondered if I had done something wrong.

Afterwards, I asked why they had laughed. I was told that the audience just liked me, which with hindsight suggests that they thought I was comically sweet, but I didn't understand that at the time, no matter how hard the grown-ups tried to explain, so I felt miserable.

Decades passed.

I made a few presentations at work, as you do. I was best man at the wedding of Martin and Alex, and also gave a speech at my own, to Harriet. I wrote journalism and books that occasionally led to appearances in front of groups of people, or on broadcast media.

Some of my talks have been scripted, others were almost entirely improvised. Some went down tremendously, others didn't. In fact, some went down very badly indeed, and you may be rather startled to read, later, what effect this had on me.

If in this book I mention some of these experiences, both good and bad, it's because I believe that we learn as much from mistakes (our own, and others') as we do from what went well. Actually, I suspect that we learn more from the mistakes.

When I worked at the *Financial Times* magazine, I was regularly teased by a colleague for putting myself into my stories. I felt slightly ashamed, but wonder now if that was only because I lacked the insight, and vocabulary, to describe why I did it. It wasn't all about showing off (though there was certainly a little of that). It was about describing situations at first-hand so that readers could imagine themselves in my place.

I don't know about you, but some readers might feel, if

they were to flick through these pages and see only stories about the giants of oratory, that they have no chance of emulating them – and give up.

I hope that, precisely because I'm a mere Gulliver in this oratorical Brobdingnag, you will reach the opposite conclusion: "If Flintoff can do it, I certainly can." To put that another way, this book contains the reflections of a fellow speaker, not the wisdom of a master to a pupil.

Odd though it may seem, it's easy to give a talk if you have no time to prepare. If you told me that you'd just been commanded to give an unplanned presentation, starting in the next five minutes, I'd say: congratulations! And if you wanted it, I'd give you some advice:

Take deep breaths before you start.

Look at your audience, and remember at all times that you are here to serve: keep the focus on them, rather than worrying about whether you are being "good" or not.

As you draw to the end, impose structure retrospectively, by summarising what you have already said.

Thank everybody for their precious time.

That's it. Simple? Yes, but only because nobody can expect you to deliver, without any notice, something amazing. It's only when you have time to prepare that it gets difficult.

Perhaps you have bought this book with only a few days to go before an important event, and are desperately flicking through, looking for ten simple bullet points that will make your speech into an instant success. While I can't make any promises, the tips I outline later on will help you to feel more confident about the task before you. But in my experience, the most memorable things I have learned about public speaking have come out of stories – some telling of great triumphs and others of getting it horribly wrong. Indeed, it's from the ones that have gone wrong that I've learnt the most, which is why I would recommend not skipping to the back at this point (however tempting it may be).

The purpose of this book is to encourage you to believe, through precept, personal experience and the stories of others, that you have a right to speak, occasionally a duty to do so, that you ought to work hard beforehand to make the best of the opportunity, but also be willing to throw away your careful preparation if circumstances call for that, and trust yourself to improvise.

## Reasons you shouldn't speak

Sometimes there are reasons you might think you shouldn't speak when you are given the opportunity. They include:

- Being afraid
- Thinking you are unworthy, or not up to it
- Worrying that you might upset people; or they won't understand you
- Not having done anything quite like it before
- Holding too tightly to a painful memory of previous occasions that went badly.

These all seem like very good reasons to avoid speaking, I'm sure, but they aren't. Let me explain.

- You should be afraid, or at least a tiny bit nervous

- There are innumerable cases of "lowly" people coming up with the goods
- Sometimes audiences need to be unsettled; and there are ways to aid comprehension
- If you won't try new things, why be alive?
- The way to move on is to put bad experiences behind you.

Good reasons not to speak include these:

- You have nothing new to say, at least for now
- Your ideas would be better shared on paper or digitally, saving the time and effort involved in attendance
- You have concluded, after careful thought, that this is not the right time for you, either because you would like longer to prepare, or you are not ready yet to share something/it will be too late
- You may be thinking, "I don't have any choice." You have been told to speak, perhaps by your employer, and you can't think of a way out of it. We'll come back to that.

## Nobody is beyond help

You can be a great speaker if you were born with a speech impediment, part lisp and part stammer; even if this requires you to avoid the treacherous rhythms of everyday speech. You can be a great speaker if your voice is unattractive, and not resonant. You can be a great speaker if you are physically ungainly – short, say, with a hunched frame, a stooping walk and a weak upper lip. If you lack the capacity to charm people, you can be a great speaker. If you have a lifelong inferiority complex because you didn't study at Oxford or Cambridge, you can be a – well, you can guess how this sentence is going to end. And you can be a great speaker if every one of these descriptions applies to you, because they all applied to Winston Churchill, and he was a great speaker.

But he worked at it. Really hard. He consulted voice specialists to improve his delivery. Studied and memorised great speeches of the past, spent many hours polishing his own, and yet more hours in front of a mirror practising gestures and facial expressions.

So it seems desperately unfair that his glittering, well-built speeches failed more often than they succeeded, over his career as a whole – because he was no good at speaking off the cuff. Too often, he was over-prepared, inflexible, ill-suited to the changing moment. Arthur Balfour – a brilliant extempore speaker – mocked Churchill's speech-making as a specimen of "powerful but not very mobile artillery".

Partly for that reason, this book will show you not only how to prepare something powerful in writing, but also how to cast it aside if the moment requires, and confidently improvise.

To do either of these things even adequately requires hard work and a willingness to take risks. Whoever you are, whatever you plan to achieve by your speaking and presenting, you must push through the ghastliness of doing it badly at first if you want to find success. It won't happen if you give up.

I know how tempting that is.

At secondary school, I went through a terrible patch. I was desperately awkward, especially around girls. I don't think I'm unique, but that was no consolation.

At fourteen, I switched from sport to drama half way through the school year. This was partly because the boys doing sport were psychopaths. When the teacher wasn't watching, which happened a lot, the boys would start playing a game called Punching Circle. It was a very simple game: just punch the next person as hard as you can on the upper arm, and they in turn must punch the next person, until it has gone all the way round.

You mustn't flinch when it's your turn to take the blow, otherwise you get punched again. (Like I said, it's a simple game.)

But my move from sport was also substantially motivated by the type of people I would be joining in drama: *tons of girls.* And drama turned out to be good for me, in so many ways. But there was one excruciating moment towards the end of the year. The drama teacher sat us in a circle and asked what we'd got out of a particular project…

"John, how did you think it went?"

(I hated people calling me John, instead of John-Paul or JP, but I'd given up correcting them.)

"All right," I replied. And then I went bright red. And the more I thought about how embarrassed I was, the more embarrassed I became. I was looking at the carpet, and I couldn't help it but my mouth kept filling up with saliva, so I had to keep swallowing, as if I was scared. And all the time the girls I liked were watching, quietly *waiting for me to say something.*

I thought I would die.

Then my eyes started to water. Staring dimly at the carpet and swallowing like a maniac, I wished I'd stayed in sport. Because the thing about the nutters was, I knew how to behave: muck about, come up with evil tricks to play on each other and throw insults.

Drama was different. Girls didn't appear to be tremendously impressed by that kind of thing.

After waiting for me to say something, and watching me go red and swallow all the time, the teacher said, "Are you feeling a little shy...?"

Oh, God.

"No," I said, and gulped some more. I looked around to see if everyone was watching me. They were, but some of them looked away to make me feel more comfortable. I didn't look closely, just glanced, but I think that the girl I liked most was staring at her hands and pretending she wasn't watching.

When the lesson ended and people started to leave the classroom, the teacher stood by the door and intercepted me. He put his arms around me and hugged me. I was astonished. I just stood there, taller than him, with my arms hanging by my sides.

He said, "John, listen, you're doing *so much* better now than when you started. *Well done.*" He said it quietly, under his breath so nobody would hear. But everybody was staring at us. He was a brilliant teacher and years later I still massively value what he said. This was just me, being weird and shy.

✦✦✦

You won't be surprised to learn that, some years later, when I first tried cold-calling, I was hopeless. By then I was studying for a degree, spending the summer in San Francisco on a student work permit. My friends had taken jobs riding tourists up and down the city's steep hills in pedicabs, or working behind the counter in a deli. But I was going to make a heap of money selling subscriptions to *Time* magazine.

Oh yes.

The job ad was very compelling. It promised an enormous commission, certainly by the standards of my income at that time. Even before I had landed the job, I could imagine myself living the high life while my friends toiled away for peanuts.

At the interview, I told the boss I had sales experience – which was a lie. My mum had always advised me not to do this. But what else to do, if you don't have experience?

He gave me some leads to call – a heap of names, addresses and phone numbers, printed on slips of thin paper. (This was before digital.)

He gave me a script, and instructions to follow it closely. Oh, and one other thing, he said: "You mustn't hang up on anybody. They can hang up on you, but not the other way round. But I'm sure I don't need to tell you that, because you English are very polite. You got a big advantage with that accent!" Then he showed me to my desk. "I'll be listening in, every so often, to see how you are doing," he said. I think this was meant to be encouraging.

I spent a little time reading the script, to internalise it. Make it seem natural. At this distance, of course, I don't remember the exact words. But I do remember thinking that I would probably subscribe to *Time* magazine myself, if somebody recited them to me with sufficient warmth and a hint of spontaneity.

By now, my new colleagues were already well into making calls. Some had even closed sales.

I hadn't even started. So I took up the receiver, ready to dial, and selected the first of my leads.

I was no expert, but the name looked Chinese. I looked at the one beneath. Also Chinese. And the one beneath that... In fact, they all appeared to be Chinese. It seemed they had been extracted from a phone directory, all from the same part of the city: Chinatown. My heart sank a little. But I had no idea, yet, how difficult this would make my job.

I started confidently, asking for the individual named on my slips of paper.

Sometimes that was the person who answered the phone, sometimes they put the receiver down to fetch someone else. And when I was sure I had the right person, I launched into my script with as much warmth as I could muster. Only to be interrupted fairly quickly by somebody speaking Chinese. I couldn't hang up, and I knew my supervisor might be listening, so I kept talking English. This had the effect of enraging the people I'd called. Not once or twice but always. And eventually they hung up on me.

I could feel my heart racing. And after a few hours of this, my confidence crumpled. I found I was making calls hunched over the phone, my voice low, so that my neighbours wouldn't hear my humiliation.

I didn't realise at the time that this posture, quiet tone and fear of humiliation made selling even more unlikely.

Between calls, I looked around at my colleagues, working their phones, and marvelled at their ability. I was particularly struck by the only other Englishman in the room – a blond chap with round John Lennon specs – who kept rising from his chair to high-five his neighbours. He was obviously doing very well. In a coffee break, I nervously asked him for his secret. He said the accent was a huge asset: "Americans love it."

But not Chinese Americans – at least, not the ones I was calling. *They* didn't love my accent. They didn't love me calling them. They wanted me to go away. At least, I think they did, but as I didn't understand a word they said, I can't be sure of that.

Not long after that, back in England, I got my first job as a journalist.

On my very first day, I was shouted at on the phone by a dozen of the most senior people in the industry I was covering. Remembering my experience (not) selling *Time* magazine subscriptions, it wasn't long before I was shaking, my knees literally knocking together.

Here's what happened. I was given a desk and a list of the top 100 law firms in London, plus a list of all the partners in each one. My job was to phone the partners at every firm and ask how their financial year had gone. I had to find out their gross turnover; profit margin; how profit was shared, and between how many partners; what junior and senior partners earned; and how long it took partners to reach the top.

There was no reason why anybody should answer my questions. It was none of my business. And lawyers, in those days, didn't talk to journalists.

My heart raced, but I picked up the phone and started

making calls. Within hours, I had spoken to hundreds of very senior lawyers. Most slammed the phone down within seconds. A few listened for a while, perhaps amused by my cheek.

For two days, that was the extent of my success. I wondered if I would be fired.

On the third day, a man at a firm I'd not heard of – but which turned out to be one of the very biggest – gasped in disbelief: "Wait a minute!" he said. "You want me to tell you how much I earn? And my partners?"

I said: Yes, please. And because I expected him to hang up, as everybody else had done, I started scanning my lists for the next person to call.

But he didn't hang up. He did something different. He gently placed the receiver down on his desk – I heard the soft tap of plastic on wood – then moved across the room towards a filing cabinet, which I heard him opening.

My heart was pounding.

He closed the drawer and came back. I heard a whump as he put down (I guessed) a heavy file. He picked up the receiver again. "What do you want to know...?"

He gave me everything. Afterwards, I sat back in my chair with immense satisfaction, and prepared to deliver this rather explosive material to my new colleagues. I felt like Churchill preparing to announce the end of the war.

## Necessary work

I mentioned earlier how hard Churchill worked on his oratory. I want to give you a greater sense of what that meant.

When he was young man, Churchill worked as a journalist. He was very good at it. He also published a novel. In short, he was an accomplished and fluent writer. But he was not good at spontaneity, and relied heavily on his writing skills when he went into politics. Dreading that he might blurt out some unpremeditated remark, he wrote his speeches as formal literary compositions, dictated in full beforehand, lovingly revised and polished, with stage directions written into his text. His first Commons speech took him six weeks to prepare. A 45-minute oration usually took him between six and eighteen hours to perfect.

David Cannadine, in his introduction to *Blood, Toil, Tears and Sweat : The Speeches of Winston Churchill*, states that "even in the darkest and busiest days of the Second World War" – by which time Churchill had been a prominent parliamentarian for decades – "he was never prepared to shirk or skimp the task of composition. Although he sometimes made speeches that were ill judged or unsuccessful, he rarely made a careless or slovenly one."

Shortly after the turn of the millennium, BBC viewers voted Winston Churchill the Greatest Briton in history. A museum devoted to him was opened by the Queen, and alongside her was one of the few people still alive who worked closely with him during World War II, Patrick Kinna. Just before the opening, I went to see Kinna at his home in Brighton. A smallish man with neatly cropped hair, he answered the door wearing neatly cropped hair, shirt and tie and a blue velvet jacket – then capered up several flights of stairs to the top floor, where he waited patiently for me, puffing heavily, to catch up.

We took our places in front of an artificial fire and a fine porcelain tea service on elegant tables that had once belonged to Churchill. "After he died, Lady Churchill said she would like to give me something that Winston had used. She sent her chauffeur with them."

Kinna was 26 when the war started. Hoping to be a parliamentary reporter, he'd enrolled after school to learn shorthand and typing. Sent to Aldershot in the general call-up, he was told he was going to France to be clerk to Major-General HRH The Duke of Windsor. "I was very pleased." He served the former King for nearly a year, but as the Germans drew near, the Duke was ordered to leave Paris immediately. Kinna received a telephone call summoning him to 10 Downing Street. "They said, 'The Prime Minister wants to see [US President Franklin] Roosevelt in the mid-Atlantic. He needs you to go with him as clerk."

Why was Kinna chosen? "If I say it myself, and I know I shouldn't, I had 150 wpm at shorthand and 90 wpm typing. I was ideal for the job."

He had no idea how hard Churchill would work him.

He set off for Scotland to join Churchill's warship, with a letter handwritten by King George VI for Churchill to present to Roosevelt. Kinna had never been on a battleship before. He had a cabin to himself, but little time to spend in it once Churchill started to thrash out the Atlantic Charter with Roosevelt. Roy Jenkins, in his biography of Churchill, notes that the Prime Minister's "dictating fluency" threatened to "smother the president in a flood of long messages". That fluency was absorbed and rendered into type by Kinna. "I was terribly busy all the time. I spent days and days typing." Kinna remembered Churchill as basically a kind person, "but if he was on the job then nothing else mattered and politeness didn't come into it."

Not long afterwards, Japan attacked Pearl Harbor, the US entered the war, and Kinna got another call from Downing Street. "I thought, 'Oh dear, what have I done wrong?' But they said the PM wanted to say how very pleased he was with my work, the speed and accuracy, and wanted me to join his staff." Considering the workload, Kinna hesitated. "I always had plenty of cheek, so I said I was flattered but needed time to think about it. I went home and spoke to my father and mother and they said it's a great honour – so I accepted."

From then on, he accompanied Churchill on each of his many overseas trips. The work was unrelenting.

"One year, we spent Christmas in the White House. Winston went to the bathroom and told his valet to send me in. So I went along, and there he was, as naked as the day he was born, getting in and out of the bath as he dictated. The poor valet was trying to dry him, but Winston wouldn't give him a chance."

Churchill habitually worked late into the night. On one occasion in Moscow, he started a meeting with Stalin at 11pm.

Kinna had a framed photograph, taken in the Kremlin, hanging in his hall. "That's Winston," he told me. "That's Averell Harriman, who came in place of Roosevelt. That's Stalin." There was one other person in the photograph: a bespectacled young man perched on the edge of the sofa with an arm stretched familiarly behind Churchill. "That's me," he said.

After the war, Churchill lost the election. As leader of the opposition, he asked to see Kinna. "He talked about the war and the places we had been and the things we had seen together. Then he asked if I would continue as his private secretary. I felt very honoured, but I was so tired, after all those years of long hours." He declined. Churchill said he understood, and wrote him a handsome testimonial.

The point of this story? Kinna worked hard. But Churchill, more than twice his age, worked even harder. If this makes your heart sink – well, fair enough. To me, it seems wonderful that Churchill was so devoted to being a great speaker.

## Compare and contrast

Forgive me, but I'm about to compare myself with Churchill. I shouldn't need to apologise, because speakers looking to explore an idea or situation routinely deploy comparison and contrast, sometimes using just a couple of phrases ("Roses are red, violets are blue") other times more expansively. It's a technique you can use yourself – you probably do it many times a day – but I mention it so particularly because I want to make clear that I don't think of myself as his equal.

It's just that I'm aware that giving only examples of exalted speakers could be off-putting and intimidating, while restricting myself to examples of people who are only adequate would be uninspiring. So, here goes...

Like Churchill, I too was a journalist at the start of my career. I too love playing with language: a word-nerd, never happier than fiddling about with a sentence. Mind you, I didn't want to be a journalist. I wanted to be a poet, and only concluded about three days after leaving university that writing poetry wouldn't be an effective way to make a living. (I thought journalism was!) I continued to write poetry, or some might say verse, in my spare time.

About ten years ago, I wrote a book about trying to avoid environmental disaster and climate change by becoming self-sufficient. Recognising that much of the discourse around this topic tended to be dismal and was heeded only by those already convinced that we're doomed, I tried to write something with wider appeal, a variously earnest and comic book about learning to make all my own clothes, which I did, dementedly, right down to the crocheted underpants. It was supposed to make people laugh, and led to me being invited to give talks here and there, initially to environmental groups, then further afield. Having by this time lost much of my early shyness, largely due to the requirement that journalists get out and talk to people, but also because I had already delivered a best-man's speech and a groom's speech, I found that I rather enjoyed giving talks.

I could pretend that I spent very little time preparing them, but that would be only partly true, because I'd already gone to the considerable trouble of writing a whole book about my topic, firmly embedding stories and ideas in my brain.

Three things in particular pleased me about my talks: people laughed (where they were supposed to, and not so far as I could tell otherwise); I received encouraging feedback from audience members and organisers; and my publisher was invited to send me to talk at a place called The School of Life.

When I first met the people in charge, Morgwn Rimel and Caroline Brimmer, sitting around a table in their basement classroom, I told them I had never heard of The School of Life. Morgwn was polite, but a flash in her eyes suggested I must have been living under a stone, because even in those relatively early days it had lots of fans and won plenty of media attention.

Despite my thoughtless remark, they kindly invited me to come back and talk about my book. It evidently went OK, because next they asked me to help create and deliver regularly a three-hour evening class on the theme of "making a difference".

Altogether, I worked with The School of Life for nearly seven years, though never full time. Even in the busiest periods, working as a visiting member of what was grandly called the faculty, I rarely did more than three events, classes or talks a month. The highlights included running an intimate John Ruskin-themed "conversation dinner", where (not knowing who he was) I stupidly gave drawing instructions to a Turner Prize winner, who was very nice about it, and found myself discussing the great Victorian with the actor Greg Wise, who had come in costume, because he was playing Ruskin in a movie at that time. Another highlight was seeing one of my favourite school teachers walk into my class (!) and confide to me at the end that I had made a decent fist of it. I was sent regularly to deliver classes inside companies that wanted to borrow a bit of The School of Life's glamour, and twice hosted the annual Christmas event, open to the ticket-buying public, alongside another faculty member who would subsequently become a friend, the broadcast journalist Tazeen Ahmad.

I had no idea, until I came to The School of Life, that I would enjoy teaching – learning and then presenting three-hour classes to a total of many thousands of people. Being insatiably curious, I wanted to teach every class there was, and I managed quite a few, from How to Have Better Conversations (riotous, at times) to How to Think about Death (challenging, but never, as you might imagine, gloomy). More than this, I was given space and time to try out my own classes.

At the end of one class, a man and woman approached me. They were about my age, but looked like lovestruck teens. The woman told me they had been to one of my classes a year previously and it had changed her life. I said I was delighted to hear it, but I felt a momentary panic at what she went on to say. She said I had asked a question that made her leave her husband.

The question I had asked, she said, was "What conversations are you not having, with yourself and with others?" I'm not going to guess how that question had such an effect on her. But it did. She said she went home, thought about it, and left her husband. Now she had a new partner – a man she had met at that same class. He was standing before me, and he too was beaming.

Another time, during a class, a woman did a reflective exercise on paper that demonstrated to her that the most important people in her life were in Australia – and promptly announced, right there and then, her determination to move to the Antipodes.

One day Caroline told me that The School of Life was

planning to publish a series of books. Would I like to write one? I said yes. What would it be, she asked?

How to Change the World, I said. (I don't know where the idea came from.)

OK, replied Caroline.

I was one of the six authors who wrote books for the series. To mark the publication, we got together to deliver the gist of our books to a large audience in London, in time slots of fifteen minutes each.

I didn't set out to do talks and classes. I stumbled into it. I took no risks setting up an event, just accepted other people's invitations. For as long as the invitations kept coming, that was fine. When they stopped, it wasn't.

But for now there was more help to come. Out of the blue, a woman living in Norway got in touch and told me she had read my book, How to Change the World, found it to be good and considered that it could help people in the country of her birth, Greece. (I still find it strange to write that sentence.)

As it happens, I told her, the book was about to be published in Greece. Great, she said. I should ask my Greek publisher to get me onto the line-up to speak at TEDx Athens, which was then (and maybe is still) the largest TED event outside California. I phoned the publisher, who duly made some calls, but TEDx Athens was only two weeks away and the line-up was fixed. Feeling obliged to this enthusiastic and supportive woman, I called her in Norway to let her know the disappointing news.

But Marie Efpraxiadis wasn't so easily put off. She contacted the organisers herself. I have no idea what she said, but suddenly I was on the line-up. I flew to Athens, was photographed and interviewed, met some wonderful people and heard that some of them found my eighteen-minute talk useful and even inspiring.

To be clear: none of this would have happened without the strong and active support of Marie. Everyone needs a Marie! But you can't ask for a Marie – she has to spontaneously present herself. This might seem like quite a conundrum. But it's actually very simple: it means we all get the opportunity, every so often, to present ourselves as a supportive, enthusiastic Marie to someone else. And, if we're lucky enough to meet a Marie ourselves, we should be prepared to accept her challenge.

Lucky us.

## Five parts of oratory

A long time before TED reached Athens, Greece was the home of oratory. Pericles kicked it off, about 2,500 years ago, when he made it clear that democracy involved discussion rather than bonking each other on the head with a stick. Soon after that, a bunch of experts sprang up, willing to teach Ancient Greeks to speak effectively (for a fee, obviously).

That's where it all started. And for centuries, people all over Europe and beyond remained nuts about the Ancient Greek structures and classifications of thought and expression that together are known as rhetoric. These structures and classifications are indeed hot stuff, but to the modern mind they have the capacity to seem Very Boring Indeed.

Introduction

So I'm not going to tell you a huge amount about rhetorical figures, much though I love them. Not in this book, anyway, but you'll find more on my website: https://flintoff. org/modest-adequate/.

All you need to know for now is this: the Greeks, then the Romans, and more or less everybody since, used a five-part process to create a speech. And I'll use it too.

These were: 1. Invention 2. Arrangement 3. Style 4. Memory, and 5. Delivery. The following pages will take you through each step. You'll see that some take more time and effort than others. You'll also see that they're not absolutely separate: you need to jump back and forward occasionally as you develop your technique.

But don't worry, it's all quite straightforward. Just try to enjoy yourself.

# INVENTION

## Work out what the heck you are up to

*Stage fright is only half the challenge for most people.*
*The other half is the Now I Have To Write It Problem.*

Peggy Noonan

Congratulations. You're giving a talk. That can only be because you already have insight and expertise. You may have the certificates to prove it, right up to a Nobel Prize. Or it may be that your expertise is precisely that you aren't an expert: you may genuinely not have a clue. If that's so, it's exactly the inexpertise that qualifies you to speak: remember the little boy in the Hans Christian Andersen story, *The Emperor's New Clothes*, who didn't know any better than to tell the Emperor the truth, that he was walking about entirely naked?

If you're a decent human being, you may possibly worry that you have nothing to offer, but you do, because you were invited to talk, or else you volunteered and somebody said yes, so the real challenge is to assess what particular impact you want to have. Apart from grabbing your audience's attention, is your aim to unsettle, or to reassure?

You can only assess that impact by first auditing (as much as possible) the interests of your audience and deciding on the specific argument you plan to make about the general subject. When these things are clear, you are ready to select your content and arrange it – but that's for the next chapter.

For now, we're going to focus on the purpose of your talk.

## The six key questions

So, start by asking yourself the following six key questions:

1. Who are you talking to? And Who, to them, are you?
2. What do you intend to talk about?
3. Why are you talking about it?
4. Where are you speaking?
5. And When? Because location and timing are crucial
6. And, bearing in mind your answers to all the above, How?

Each of these questions tends to produce, as well as answers, additional queries. The following mind map gives a sense of what some of these might be.

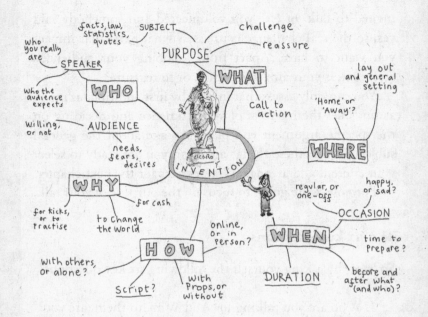

facts, law, statistics, quotes

SUBJECT

challenge

reassure

who you really are

SPEAKER

PURPOSE

WHAT

Who the audience expects

WHO

Call to action

lay out and general setting

'Home' or 'Away'?

Willing, or not

AUDIENCE

needs, fears, desires

INVENTION

Cicero

WHERE

WHY

regular, or one-off

happy, or sad?

for kicks, or to practise

for cash

to change the world

online, or in person?

OCCASION

WHEN

time to prepare?

with others, or alone?

HOW

with props, or without

DURATION

before and after what (and who)?

Script?

## Who are you talking to?

It's important to acknowledge immediately that an audience is not a single entity, but a group of individuals who differ from one another perhaps as much as they may differ from you. If you forget that, the slip is unlikely to work in your favour.

Another point to consider is that, in many cases, you will be talking to more than one audience at once. Not only because there is more than one interest group in the room, but because there are others outside who are important to you. In a general election, party leaders frequently find themselves speaking to a gathering of factory workers, or a local branch of their party, but the real audience they are hoping to convince is the ordinary voter watching highlights on the TV news, or on social media. Needless to say, this doesn't only apply to politicians. Perhaps the event where you are speaking is being transmitted live for people elsewhere to watch and listen to in real time, or later. When thinking about your audience, you need to understand how important those distant observers are, and what you can do to take them into account.

## Total strangers

If you stand on a street corner and address passers-by, you won't have much sense of what makes them tick. Nor can you expect a lot of goodwill from them, because many people assume that if you speak in public like that you're either bonkers or will shortly be asking them for money (or both).

Long before I dreamed of writing a book about how to change the world, I wrote a magazine story for *The Sunday Times* about political apathy. I met lots of people, who all had moderately interesting things to say, but none of it was thrilling. My editor suggested I take a soap box to a crowded place, stand on it and make a speech about the topic. I laughed, then realised she was entirely serious, so I did what she suggested.

I confess that I felt rather nervous. I phoned my father, who as well as being an actor has been actively involved in politics, and asked for tips. He suggested I just step up and say something like 'Ladies and Gentlemen, if I could just have a minute of your time...'

I did as he suggested. People listened politely, even

occasionally asked me questions, and though I retained a little gathering before me for a while, it was made up of different people, coming and going as they went from being initially interested to subsequently bored.

It has been observed that most of the preaching of Jesus Christ, in the gospels, took place outdoors, and that much of it was brief. Even the longest of the parables would have taken less than five minutes. I could have learned a lot if I'd considered this before getting on my soap box.

Another time, years later, my friend Steve Chapman – a tremendous creative risk-taker – decided to busk with guitar and harmonica at London's South Bank, to launch his self-published book about creativity and risk-taking. He took along a sign offering free copies of the book for anybody who wanted one, and boxes full of pristine first editions. He deliberately refused to rehearse or even imagine what he might do when he got there. I went along to give him moral support, and film the proceedings. (I was "doing a Marie".)

I noticed that when Steve sang soulfully about himself, or about the contents of his book, people tended to stay away, but when he picked up the tempo and loudly repeated his simple refrain, "Book launch! Book launch!", they were drawn in. He had discovered that engaging with strangers calls for high energy, maximum volume and a simple message. He could have learned as much by talking to the proprietor of any fruit and veg stall, but that would not have been so exciting.

Despite what I said a little earlier, no crowd is a total mystery, not even passing strangers. In the examples I have given, the speakers could make some large assumptions based on time and location.

A high proportion of Steve's passers-by were probably tourists, tourists who liked the idea of creativity (why else come to the South Bank?). If he paid attention to their outfits he could guess that the ones wearing suits and walking faster than the ones in brightly coloured shorts were probably working Londoners on a lunch break. If he'd wanted to know more, he could ask them (he did).

Why does this matter? Because you can never know too much about your audience. The more detail you gather, the more you can be confident that what you are saying isn't an unfathomable mystery to them, or horribly offensive.

Somebody who spoke a lot outdoors was the political playwright George Bernard Shaw. At university, I was a big Shaw fan, and enthusiastically consumed all four volumes of Michael Holroyd's biography. I was mesmerised by Shaw's commitment, not unlike Churchill's, to public speaking.

Over the course of a decade, Shaw gave more than a thousand talks. Unlike Churchill, Shaw delivered without a script, but he did carry a series of prompt cards, covering a variety of subjects.

Naturally shy, Shaw used street-corner oratory to learn how to address an audience, "as a man learns to skate or to cycle, by doggedly making a fool of myself until I got used to it". He spoke in workmen's clubs, coffee houses, to secular societies and radical associations, wrote Holroyd. "He preferred speaking in the open air at all sorts of holes and corners – under lamp posts, at dock gates, in parks, squares, marketplaces – and in all sorts of weather."

One of his finest talks, Shaw recalled, was given in a downpour at Speakers Corner in Hyde Park to a small group of policemen. "I spoke very well in my effort to convert them [to socialism]," he recalled. And conversion, rather than mere entertainment, was always his aim. "My platform performances are for use, not for ornament."

## Captive strangers

This kind of audience has not chosen to be with you, and may feel trapped. Unlike the people who gathered around Steve's wild singing, at London's South Bank, this audience may feel unable to leave. Shaw's policemen, for all his satisfaction, may have taken no great pleasure in hearing him bang on about socialism, at least not initially, but he was an entertaining speaker and probably won them round.

It's worth being aware in advance of the resentment that a captive audience may feel towards you. The only solution is to build, as fast as you can, a sense of what they want, what they fear, and what they need – as you should with any audience – and address that directly.

In my experience, this kind of audience has included inmates in prisons, who attended only because it got them out of their cells for a while; children in schools, who had no idea who I was and couldn't care less; and employees in companies who felt they had no say in the choice of entertainment, training or whatever it was I had been summoned to provide.

I sympathise with them all, because I myself have felt like a captive stranger occasionally. For instance, at weddings when a speaker was not thinking of the audience as a whole but sharing insider jokes with only a small part of it; and in news conferences at big newspapers where, as a relatively junior reporter, I quickly became bored listening to the know-it-all banter between senior editors and wondered if I was the only person feeling that way (I wasn't).

## Potential customers

Potential customers, if you understand your market, have none of the indifference of street-corner passers-by and, unlike captive strangers, they know that listening to you is optional. For all that, they may actually be more sceptical and hostile than either of the previous types, especially if they suspect that you only want their money.

## Colleagues

Colleagues are rarely your equals, because most workplaces are hierarchical, even when they pretend they're not. It's one thing addressing the people you report to. It's another thing addressing the people who report to you. And it's another thing again if they're all in the same room together. None of these situations is "better" or "worse" than the other – they're neither good nor bad. But you do need to understand what the situation is, and the audience's expectations.

## Existing customers

Like potential customers, the ones who already pay you may be demanding and even unpleasant. The difference is that existing customers will not ignore you – unless you have already done what they expected from you, or failed to do it, in which case being ignored may mean they do not intend to continue being your customer.

## True believers

This is an audience to which you yourself belong, as when campaigners speak to activists, politicians rally party supporters, preachers preach to the, er, converted. Assuming that the speaker is not some kind of cult leader (see: Fans, below), everybody is more or less equal. This means that they can disagree fiercely among themselves. For instance, sects within the same religion might go to war because some believe this, while others believe that; and in political parties, individual members are never forgiven by their fellows for voting the "wrong" way on issues that an outsider would quickly forget.

## *Your peers*

In some situations, it is possible to come together as peers, with a genuinely flat structure. This generally requires prior agreement from all participants, and careful set-up, but it's not difficult.

In a situation like this, it becomes easier to let down your guard and admit to uncertainty and mistakes. Not long ago, I helped to organise a group of authors who came together as equals to talk candidly about publishing in a safe space. Having agreed that anybody could ask anything, and that participants could freely join or quit any discussion at any time without offence, we had an amazingly honest conversation. Partly for that reason, it was an experience that created strong bonds between the participants.

Another context in which you might speak to your peers is in the meetings of Toastmasters, the international movement where individuals meet to polish up their public speaking in front of each other; or at any of the 12-step fellowships (not just Alcoholics Anonymous) where people gain experience, strength and hope by sharing their common problems and triumphs.

## Your fans

Fans might sound like a wonderful thing to have, but they can be problematic too. The main thing to be careful about is taking this audience for granted. Another difficulty can arise when you try something that doesn't fit with your fans' fixed ideas about you, and it doesn't go down well. In situations like this, the person who feels trapped may be you.

## What do you intend to talk about?

Another way to understand your audience is to think about its needs, hopes and fears. These are reasons why people will listen to you – or not.

Sometimes the reasons are not what you think they are.

I was once invited to give a talk about *How to Change the World* to a group of people at a massive technology company. I was excited, but didn't really think much about what I was going to do until a couple of weeks beforehand. And it suddenly dawned on me that this particular group of people in this particular company were already harnessing their talents to changing the world, and could have taught me more than I could ever tell them. It didn't make sense. Panicking a little, I contacted the man who had invited me to speak, and made an appointment to come in and explain my confusion.

I asked him directly: "How do you want the people in the room to be changed, no matter how much or how little, by this talk?"

Forced to think it through, he agreed that it was silly

for me to tell them what they already knew. He talked a bit about his own needs, hopes and fears. He said that the individuals in his team tended to be perfectionists, so they never allowed themselves to make mistakes, which drastically affected their willingness to be creative. He said it took on average eight interviews to get a full-time job at his company, and practically every individual believed that their colleagues were all geniuses, while they themselves were frauds, and had only been hired by accident. He said they tended to work in isolation, so there was little team spirit. And that, despite his efforts to be friendly, most seemed intimidated by him. What he really wanted was to bring individuals together to be entertained; to bond with each other, and with him.

This helped a lot. I went away and cooked up a plan.

So when you come to planning your talk, think of your audience. Try to find out what they need, what they're hoping for. Consider what they have actually told you. Some will have been direct, while others may have addressed their interests only obliquely.

What might Steve's passers-by have needed? Tourists need entertainment, and a story to tell when they go home. At the South Bank, they hope for something quintessentially British, and artistic. They might be afraid of being ripped off in a foreign country, or of being delayed unduly on their way to a pre-planned tourist highlight elsewhere.

Authors who came to the event about publishing needed help understanding the rapid changes in the industry, and a place where they could speak honestly and ask questions they couldn't ask anybody else. They hoped to find answers, and to help answer each other's questions. Some, it turned out, had been afraid that the day would be a monumental waste of time. Others may have feared speaking honestly.

As well as asking people, you can look at what they have said or written elsewhere. Again, try to look beyond the obvious. If people say they want to lose weight, is that what they really want? It could be that they want to look slim. It could be that they're afraid of having a heart attack and dying. Or both. There's no way to be entirely sure, but by asking yourself the question you have a better chance to be of service to them.

The organisers of the event in Mexico had asked me to record a video message before I flew out, to give people a taste of what was to come. I had absolutely no idea about my audience – I didn't even know if they were native Mexicans or outsiders flying in. But I could see that recording a video was an excellent idea, and I have subsequently done it many times.

By recording some kind of greeting, I've often encouraged the people I will be meeting to introduce themselves – to me and to each other.

Sometimes, their messages have included a detailed sense of what they are looking to get out of the occasion. For several years in a row, I've taught would-be authors on residential retreats, and one time I sent out a welcome video in advance, with a mechanism for people to reply to me and to each other. This rapidly accelerated the bonding process, which usually takes a few days, because even on first meeting the participants weren't entirely strangers.

I built on this idea, subsequently, when a book club more

than a hundred miles away invited me to visit. I couldn't justify the time, but suggested joining them onscreen instead, and sent a little personalised video asking what they might like me to talk about. This was before the lockdown of 2020, and meeting online was much less familiar to most people. All the same, several individuals replied with interesting questions about the writing process, so I made a few additional, simple videos answering their questions, which I posted online. This seemed to go down satisfactorily, and when the time came for our actual online gathering, it felt like I was joining friends. You might think that this sounds like a lot of work, but the videos I recorded for that book club are ready and waiting for anybody else who might pop along another time.

✦ ✦ ✦

At the start of this book, I mentioned a seasoned author who dreaded his first-ever online book launch, to a paying audience he wouldn't be able to see. He'd watched other authors – really famous ones, he mentioned them by name – and said it was dreadful, embarrassing to watch them rhubarbing into the void. He told me this during the 2020 pandemic, when an online launch for his own book was the only option.

Having tried it myself, I was able to recommend that he do a pre-recorded video, asking for questions and comments in advance from people who would attend his talk. Then, in the launch itself, he could acknowledge those questions and comments, creating a rapport with those invisible watchers.

It wasn't a very ingenious idea. It wasn't original to me. But he looked immensely grateful to have it. A few weeks later, I attended somebody else's online book launch. This author had not created a pre-recorded video, but the problem of how to engage with the strangeness of an online audience – physically distant, but with a clear view up your nostrils – was managed by having one friendly guest interview the author, making what could have been a lecture into a more intimate conversation. This is an idea you could borrow, whether you speak online or in person.

## Why are you talking about it?

A common mistake for beginners is to think first – or only – about the general subject of a speech or talk. But before thinking about your subject you must understand your particular argument about that subject (your angle, your take on it). And before thinking about your argument, you must consider your purpose – the impact you want to have.

Let me give an example. In Shakespeare's *Henry V*, there's a rousing speech before a battle in which the king successfully injects courage into his outnumbered troops.

The king's subject is, I suppose, being outnumbered. Or it could be "on being brave". Or even "today is Saint Crispin's day". None of them especially motivating.

His argument is roughly: this is Saint Crispin's day, and you'll never forget it if you come through this alive, because you'll be covered in glory, unlike all those cowards back home who didn't come with us. A bit better.

His purpose: to motivate.

When you read it like this, you see that it's necessary to do it the other way around. Figure out your purpose first, before you devise your argument, and only then choose your subject, which (it turns out) can be any old thing, even including the patron saint of cobblers, if today happens to be his day.

Starting with your subject is not just a common mistake but, as this example suggests, it can also be a dangerous one: if King Henry supposed that his key task was to master his subject, he'd have spent hours swotting up on Saint Crispin and the art of making shoes. His troops would have been baffled by his speech and would probably have been slaughtered.

Save lives! Approach your speech in this order:

- Purpose – what you want to achieve
- Argument – how you will persuade people
- Subject – whatever you can use.

When my drama teacher asked how I was getting on, I had no subject, no argument and no purpose (except to avoid speaking, but that was impossible). Cold-calling in California, I had a subject, *Time* magazine, and an argument that had been scripted by somebody else, to the effect that subscribing to this magazine could alter a person's life for the better in ways they probably couldn't even imagine, and that now was the time to do it, because I was able to offer them a discount. My purpose, however, was just to earn money: I was totally disconnected from the interests of both *Time* magazine and the benighted individuals who had the misfortune to take my call. And on my first day as a journalist, my subject was "the financial performance of law firms this year", my argument was that it was in everybody's interest for *Legal Business* magazine to publish the figures, and my purpose was to find out some of those figures, because I wanted to keep my job, because by then I really wanted to be a journalist.

Even if you're doing a talk with a function that seems incredibly obvious, because it's been done a zillion times before, you should always do this exercise.

Let's say you're giving a best wo/man's speech at a wedding. I hope that you have some sense by now of the audience: at least roughly what kind of world view the relatives and friends have. What are your purpose, argument and subject?

Purpose: to move people to tears of joy? Tears of laughter? To explain the weirdness of the particular wedding ceremony? To raise funds for the honeymoon?

Argument: marriage isn't new, but it's (probably) never been tried by this particular couple before.

Subject: two people getting married. The institution of marriage generally. How these two met. Anything at all, really, so long as it fits the purpose and argument.

✸ ✸ ✸

During the Covid-19 epidemic, when masses of people around the world were getting used to delivering presentations online, I spoke to two people who had given speeches while it was still possible to do so in person, in a crowded room. We spoke remotely, by video. I'd not met either of them before, but they spoke freely and with much warmth about their experiences.

The first, Rebecca Twomey, had volunteered to be "father of the bride" for her friend's wedding. As a journalist, she was naturally comfortable with words, but told me she soon realised that speaking is not the same as writing.

Chris Toumazis, the second wedding speaker I talked to, had paired up with his brother to be joint MCs at their sister's wedding.

At first glance, their assignments might look very similar. But the tiny differences between them are crucial. Speaking about a sister is not the same as speaking about a friend you didn't meet till you were in your twenties.

Wanting most of all to deliver a good speech for her friend, who had recently been diagnosed with cancer, Rebecca was honest enough to admit to other considerations too: "I do have an ego! My ex-boyfriend might have watched the video."

Chris and his brother likewise had to find a purpose that balanced a variety of considerations: to please their sister, no traditionalist, but also her groom, who wanted the occasion to have weight. On top of that, it was important to make people laugh: "In our family, being funny is a big thing," Chris told me.

What does this have to do with you? You may have been told to do a speech or presentation, for work. You don't want to do it, and you feel lost. If that's the case, take the time to identify your purpose. Then think of the argument that will help you to achieve that. It needn't be a "big" purpose. It could be "to do the talk with as little preparation as possible without getting myself fired". Even that is a clear purpose.

If you do not have a particular speech or presentation to make in the near future, and feel unable to answer, I suggest you think instead of a conversation you need or would like to have. It could be a conversation about work, or something in your private life. It could be something that will change your life for ever, or something relatively insignificant. It doesn't matter. Whatever it is, it will have a subject, an argument and a purpose. If it doesn't, you should avoid that conversation.

To summarise: as raw ingredients are to a recipe, so is your subject to your argument. And your argument is to your purpose as a recipe is to a feast. Nobody feasts on a recipe and raw ingredients.

### Bold and creative

Some people, by now, may be feeling stuck. Identifying a subject is easy, but being clear about your argument and your purpose requires boldness and creativity. Your brain is likely to start telling you that you've done something "wrong".

That's the trouble with creative work, but also the joy of it. It's fundamentally risky, because it's revealing and subjective. Other people will get a glimpse of the kind of person you are! And they may not like it!

It's time to tell you about the Inuit walrus-tusk carvers.

Before the Enlightenment, most people believed that their talent was God-given. Since then, as large numbers of people have given up on God, the common view is that we ourselves are individually responsible for our creative victories – and defeats. An insight into how much more restful it must have been previously is provided by the story of Western anthropologists who visited Inuit settlements before they became westernised. The anthropologists were surprised to find that everybody they met was an artist. They all carved walrus tusks. Sometimes the carving was very good. At other times, it was so-so. But so-so carvings weren't embarrassing to the people who delivered them to the world, because they believed that "God didn't put a good carving in that tusk".

If you have been struggling to come up with an argument and a purpose for your speech or presentation, I recommend that you pretend for a moment to be an Inuit walrus-tusk carver, and hand over the responsibility to God. If you already believe that God is in charge, this will be easy. If you don't, simply *pretend* that God is in charge.

Throw caution aside, and allow yourself to be boldly creative.

Specifically, come up with an argument that is a) as controversial as you can manage, while also being b) true to yourself. It must be something that somebody, somewhere, might disagree with, perhaps strongly.

Thus, somebody at a wedding, a skulking onlooker, might conceivably argue that there's nothing special about this particular couple: your job is to come up with an argument proving them wrong.

As this suggests, it can be positively helpful to have in mind an "adversary" who holds a view directly at odds with your own. You don't need to hate this adversary, who might anyway be entirely hypothetical; if you are a gentle soul you might prefer to think that you're in the business of kindly putting them right, the silly sausage. But without the sense of a clear argument to push against, you're likely to drift, a sailing boat without wind in the sails. You'll have nothing to say, and you'll say nothing.

The Ancient Greeks knew how important it is to understand your adversary, and carried out rhetorical exercises to make that really obvious. I'll be coming back to rhetoric as a device for improving the style of what you say in a later chapter; but what's often forgotten is that rhetoric was originally not only a means to express ideas and opinions – it was also about how you find your ideas and opinions in the first place. The Greeks gained a deeper understanding of an issue by forcing themselves to consider it sincerely from the angle of their opponent. This served to strengthen their own argument, or to help parties find a compromise. Either way, it gives you greater clarity, which should also give you greater confidence.

## Where, and When?

David Kendall, a retired bank manager from York, arrived in Cambridge at three in the afternoon and went straight to bed in the room reserved for him at Downing College. After a couple of hours he got up, showered and dressed. Then he came downstairs for a drink, and to talk to me about his current job as a freelance after-dinner speaker, before that evening's gala.

At the bar, he ordered iced water. No alcohol, because he was driving home afterwards. "I like to get back. There's only the wife, now, and the dog." (His children have left home.) "I used to drink – but if you do that you tend to think you're funnier than you are. Then you wake up in the morning and think, 'That lady over there wasn't laughing, and nor was that man over there,' and so on. This is my job. Would you go to work on a drink?"

Taking his glass to a table, Kendall pulled a diary from his briefcase and opened it. Inside, there was a list of the occasions where he'd appeared as the after-dinner speaker. At the top of each page was the name of the organisation, the date and the venue. Already this week he'd done Nestlé in York, a computer company near Slough and, the night before, an NHS dinner in Manchester. The next day he would be in St Andrews to address the Rotary Club.

Flicking through the pages, Kendall randomly selected an event: management consultants in Aberdeen. Beneath this heading he'd handwritten key words indicating which material he used on that occasion, to help him avoid repeating himself if he were to address the same client again. (He has many similar volumes at home.)

Another precaution, he told me, is to ask his host during dinner what the organisation does, who the "characters" are, and whether certain things might be taboo. "One of my tenets is never to upset anyone."

And when dessert arrives, he excuses himself: "I go and have a pee and a cigarette, and walk around the room a bit, thinking."

❦ ❦ ❦

The timing of your talk can make a huge difference. It may come too soon for you to mention something important that won't be ready yet, or too late to mention something else that is over and done with. It's unlikely that you will be able to foresee all the implications of the date, and others will only creep up on you as the time approaches, but it's important to make a note of any advantages it gives you, as well as any disadvantages. This could significantly affect your choice of material and what you decide to leave out.

Apart from the date, there is the timing on the day. Are you the first person to speak? The last? Or will you come in the middle somewhere? How will this affect the mood of the audience? Will they be eager and excited or drained and ready to leave?

Who else is speaking, and what will they speak about? As I learned in Mexico, it's quite possible that those who speak before you will cover your material. Find out as much as you can about what they are planning.

Location is also important. If you are in Greece speaking English, as I was, you should speak more slowly than I did, because I rattled through my talk and afterwards I kicked myself, because some poor translator was simultaneously interpreting – I must have made it difficult, and perhaps even lost people.

Additionally, the location is important because it helps you to decide what kind of talk you should do. A small room with a smallish audience calls for a relatively intimate delivery, much nearer to an ordinary conversation than a speech to 50 people or more in a hall – let alone to a crowd of thousands in a stadium.

I always ask what the layout will be. Because I tend to use interaction, I prefer there to be no barriers between me and the audience. I like a semicircle best. Otherwise, seats arranged in rows, as in the theatre, with plenty of space for individuals to get up and move about. What I like least is an audience sitting behind tables: in my experience, they never really engage fully. It's not (necessarily) that they refuse to engage, or don't want to: the furniture simply gets in the way and doesn't allow it. They might as well be hiding behind a wall. (I'll come back to this.) If you can change the layout: great. If you can't, it still helps to be aware of that in advance.

Similarly, you might want to know how big the stage is, if there is one, what the sound is like and whether there's a screen, if you have something important to show people. (Generally, I avoid using slides.)

One thing I've noticed is that many organisations assume that everybody who comes in to speak will do exactly the same thing, regardless of whether any of them actually likes it. Recently I gave a talk that relied heavily on some of my drawings being projected on a screen. The only way for me to stand out of the way of the screen was either to sit behind a table or stand behind a lectern. As I said, I don't like barriers between me and the people I'm talking to – I really feel uncomfortable. So these were not attractive options. I kicked myself for not getting a clearer sense of the "stage" area beforehand, and for failing to turn up with sufficient time to get the table or lectern moved.

In 2020, in the midst of the pandemic, when events could only take place online, I found myself delivering talks into the void, to people I couldn't even see. It would be hard to imagine a greater barrier, but I mention this because the talks went surprisingly well: there is no absolute rule about what works.

Location and venue may also help you to think about

whether to use props. Steve Chapman rightly concluded that a pavement on London's South Bank, beside the Thames, was a good spot for playing guitar and harmonica and singing. It wouldn't have worked so well in a corporate meeting room behind a lectern.

There's another thing to consider about the time and place: will it affect what you ask your audience to do, when you have finished speaking?

## How?

The more specific you can be about what you want your audience to do, the easier it will be to find a way to achieve it.

I wanted the lawyers I phoned, on my first day as a journalist, to give me all their firms' confidential financial information, immediately.

Steve Chapman wanted people to take away a free copy of his book and read it.

It's hard to guess precisely what David Kendall wanted to achieve by his lugubriously funny after-dinner entertainments, but I imagine that when he heard somebody lost to hysterics he felt he had got near it.

And you? Can you specify a simple and immediate action you'd like your audience to take? Is your aim more diffuse? Is your aim, like that of Kendall and most people who give wedding speeches, to make the audience laugh and be happy? The more specific your purpose is, the more certain you can be that you have succeeded (or not).

Rachel Ison, a young psychologist, told me recently about her first "proper" experience of public speaking. It was still fresh in her mind, and I wanted to know how she came up with the idea, what she was doing it for, how she set about it and how it went.

"I wanted to do something meaningful around the time of my birthday," she told me, sitting in the canteen at the Royal Free Hospital in north London. "I'd just started volunteering for a charity called The Listening Place, and I was overwhelmed by their amazing work: ongoing, face-to-face support for adults who no longer feel that life is worth living. I was involved with the volunteering, I loved the work, and I knew that fundraising was important. So I decided I could do a relaxed fundraiser at home with people I knew: friends, my parents' friends, and family."

She was in the kitchen with her mother when she first gave utterance to the idea of a "Talk Saves Lives" themed afternoon tea. "When I said I wanted to do it, she said, 'Great, let's go.' And that was it. We wrote a little outline and sent out an invitation."

You should by now have a good sense of her purpose (raising a specific amount of money, which I'll come back to, and raising awareness). This sense of purpose (her Why) would help as she wrote her speech about talking to save lives (her What). But Who was she talking to? When, Where and How?

"I could have opened it up to a wider circle of people I didn't know very well, but it didn't feel like that type of event. I wanted it to be an intimate afternoon tea with people I knew, talking about something important to me, as opposed to 'Let's get everyone we know in a room and try and raise some money'."

Do you see how further clarity helps to focus the purpose?

As noted above, Who does not apply only to the audience. Ask yourself, who is the speaker to this audience? Ison wanted to raise money, and awareness, not just have any old birthday party. So she wanted to make it clear that she was speaking not just as a family member, her mother's daughter, but specifically as one of the charity's volunteers. She wanted to sound well informed. So she contacted The Listening Place, asked for some stats and whatever else they normally provide to people who want to do fundraising, such as leaflets and books, and started writing.

## Free speech, really?

In the country where I live, England, there have been times when saying the wrong thing could have got your head cut off. Currently, the law provides no instance of prohibited utterance that could lead to such a grim eventuality. Of course, that might change, but for now it should provide a small crumb of comfort. What's the worst that could happen? Not that.

Less drastic, but still a real restriction, are the assortment of other ways in which free expression has been constrained even here, in a country that boasts of being a longstanding champion of liberty and democracy. In theatres, within living memory, actors were not permitted to deviate from the previously authorised script, vetted by government officials in the ancient office of Lord Chamberlain. Improvisation on stage was literally illegal.

It would be easy to feel complacent about this, to

congratulate ourselves that we are finally free to say whatever we like, but of course that's not the case, as Kendall noted. Every group has its particular codes and taboos. Social norms change with startling speed, so to attempt to identify one particular example feels hazardous, like attempting to catch a bullet with my teeth. But here goes... Within 50 years of homosexuality being decriminalised, in the second half of the 20th century, it became socially unacceptable to speak of people who are heterosexual as "normal". Quite right too, you might think, and you might even say so, loudly, because at the time of writing this would place you among "right-thinking" people. If you disagree, you will probably keep that to yourself rather than start a wildfire of anger and disgust, perhaps even the loss of your employment for having crossed a line and brought your employer into disrepute, as they say on this kind of occasion.

I don't want to get bogged down in the merits of either argument, just to observe that there are always things you might believe that others, though not all others, will tell you should never be uttered aloud.

If they tell you that, you must think very hard about how to proceed. My general view is that you should say what you honestly believe, after thinking it through carefully. If you then discuss it with someone else, you may adjust your view slightly, or even entirely. If it only confirms your view, and you have sincerely thought about it with an open mind, then the world probably needs to hear what you have to say. After all, it was only through the courage of a few lonely voices that homosexuality came, eventually, to be decriminalised; and the same applies to every other instance of social change.

Speaking against received wisdom is one thing. Speaking against the law is another. Still today, you can be prosecuted in most democracies for making certain kinds of statement. Beware!

## Don't be a coward

While I was writing this, I received a call from somebody seeking advice about a problem at work. A junior member of staff, showing initiative, had done something that was not helpful, as intended, but positively inconvenient. My caller wondered what to do about it.

I suggested saying thank you, offering congratulations on having shown initiative, and adding that you'd prefer it was not done quite the same way next time.

"But I don't want to upset her."

This is often the reason we don't say what we think, whether to a subordinate at work or to a large audience anywhere. It's not a good reason. For a start, you can't possibly know what will upset another person. Secondly, being upset (if it happens) is something you can help to clear up. Thirdly, the consequences of saying nothing are too horribly predictable.

By failing to say the truth, my caller would in effect be telling her junior colleague to do the same again next time. Which would start a gradual build-up of resentment, like limescale in a kettle. Minutes, even hours, would be spent obsessively going over how annoying and stupid it all was, not least how stupid it was not to correct the error in the first place. As my caller became more annoyed by her own mistake in failing to correct it, the resentment would build up even more, and an iciness would grip their working relationship. The younger person would probably start gossiping about her boss, spreading ill will and biting into productivity. It would become necessary to cut the number of employees, and the young person whose initiative had started the whole problem would be told she had to go because she had been making the same stupid decision again and again.

She would leave, burning with rage at the injustice, never having been told she was doing anything wrong, and my friend, the caller, would be consumed with guilt. An employment tribunal would award an enormous compensation payment, destroying the company's financial health and leaving everybody out of work.

All because my friend was afraid of upsetting somebody.

Mind you, I didn't say any of this on the phone. Instead, I pointed out that it must surely be possible to deliver the message without malice, in a spirit of kindness.

She said she would try.

The point of this elaborate fantasy is that sometimes, even when you have carefully considered the nature of your audience, its needs, hopes and fears, you will choose to deliver a message that may not be welcome. After all, a good speaker can either meet an audience's expectations, or dash them. You must be willing to do both.

There's a magnificent story about a speaker turning on his audience, and it's true. I'll tell you the story, then I'll tell you how the audience responded.

Frederick Douglass, a former slave, travelled widely around the US speaking for abolition. In 1852, abolitionists in Rochester, New York, invited Douglass to speak on

Independence Day, 4th July. He was outraged, and let them know it.

"I am not included within the pale of this glorious anniversary! Your high independence only reveals the immeasurable distance between us... The blessings in which you this day rejoice are not enjoyed in common. The rich inheritance of justice, liberty, prosperity and independence bequeathed by your fathers is shared by you, not by me. The sunlight that brought life and healing to you has brought stripes and death to me. The Fourth of July is yours, not mine. You may rejoice, I must mourn... To drag a man in fetters into the grand, illuminated temple of liberty, and call upon him to join you in joyous anthems were inhuman mockery and sacrilegious irony. Do you mean, citizens, to mock me by asking me to speak today?"

In short, he gave them a proper wigging.

You might think they would be affronted by his ingratitude, hiss and whistle at him, perhaps even throw rotten veg. But no: when he finished, Douglass was greeted with universal applause.

Similarly, when the teenage Swedish climate campaigner Greta Thunberg visited New York to berate, scold, rebuke, lecture, censure, chide, reproach and dish out hard stares to the oldies at the United Nations – they loved it.

If you have the best interests of your audience at heart, kicking up dust can be a kindness. The late British rabbi Hugo Gryn used to tell students at rabbinical college: "A rabbi whose congregation does not want to run him out of town is no rabbi. And a rabbi whose congregation does run him out of town is no man."

## Writing an outline

When I was starting out as a journalist, I met a man called Brian Jenner. He was about my age, and had a terrifically loud, high-pitched laugh. He too was starting out as a journalist: we were introduced by a mutual friend, and saw each other a couple of times, socially, as part of a larger group.

I forgot about Brian for a few years, until I saw an advertisement in the back of the satirical magazine *Private Eye*, in which he advertised his services as a speechwriter. I was curious, and if I'm honest I was also slightly jealous, but I couldn't have explained why, because by that time I was doing well enough for myself, having landed my dream job as feature writer for the magazine of a national newspaper.

Then I forgot about Brian again, for about 20 years.

By a weird coincidence, just as I started writing this book, Brian popped up again. Well, maybe it wasn't really a coincidence, considering my subject matter. It turned out that while I had been not-thinking about him Brian had set up an international network of speechwriters. It looked jolly impressive. I sent him a message saying hullo, and we spoke on the phone. I was pleased to note, holding the phone away from my ear, that Brian had done nothing to hide his distinctive laugh. And even more pleased when he generously invited me to attend a conference of speechwriters in Paris.

I went along, and I learned a lot.

In particular, I learned that I can be a bit of a twit, having become a little resistant to fully preparing my speeches, after falling in love a few years ago with improvising. I'd been telling myself, for a while now, that to turn up with a prepared/written speech is to ignore the needs and wishes of the moment; and when I learned that Balfour mocked Churchill for his over-preparedness I felt justified: I was right to believe this. Improvising is always best.

I'll come back to the freedom that comes from improvisation very shortly, but for now I want to stress that I no longer believe it's unnecessary to write a speech. Far from it. In fact, I think it's absolutely necessary, even if you decide to ignore it when you come to speak, because the act of writing the speech will help you to understand what you really think.

One of the best modern speechwriters is Philip Collins. He's written an excellent book on the subject, which I've frequently consulted, and was a keynote speaker at one of Brian's international conferences. Formerly speechwriter to Tony Blair, Collins knows what he's talking about, and I sat up when he described his writing process:

Start by summarising your speech in a sentence. Don't rush this. Get it right.

Then expand the idea to fill a whole paragraph. You'll see what facts you need, and the balance of past, present and future required in your reasoning.

Take it up to a whole page. This should cover all that needs saying and no more. Test it against your one-sentence summary.

Write a detailed and thorough outline.

Take the outline to a full draft.

In his book, Collins goes through this process step by step, to create an entirely hypothetical speech. As a writer, I found it fascinating, because I have never worked that way, so I wanted to try it. For my own benefit, I wrote the proposal for this book using exactly this method.

"Get the main argument right, and you cannot write a bad speech. Get it wrong, and you cannot write a good one," he argues, using a fine specimen of the rhetorical figure known as antithesis. (Go ahead, read it again. Notice how pleasingly balanced and plausible it sounds.)

Before we move on to Chapter 2 (Arrangement), here's another thought about how to handle the rigidity of a prepared, written speech: you can change it, right up to the last minute.

Another book I have enjoyed is the *Penguin Book of Modern Speeches*, edited by the late Brian MacArthur. The speeches may be "modern", but most of the speakers anthologised in it are, like the author, sadly no longer with us. One exception, and long may he remain with us, is Neil Kinnock, the former leader of Britain's Labour Party.

Kinnock is often remembered for a speech that he got horribly, horribly wrong. At an election rally, when it looked as if he might take Labour into Downing Street, he spoke to his supporters in a kind of improvised call-and-response that might possibly have been tremendous in the hall with him, but looked terrible – smug, embarrassing – on the evening news. He lost the election.

But on a different occasion, Kinnock addressed his party conference with a speech that impressed even his foes. As usual, he'd prepared the speech earlier, but he decided to amend it in the taxi on the way to deliver it. Nobody remembers what the rest of the speech was about, but his last-minute additions, about being "the first Kinnock in a thousand generations" to achieve this and that, was beautifully judged, full of rhythm and passion. It was those last-minute additions that got him into MacArthur's anthology.

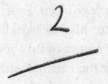

# ARRANGEMENT

## Choose really interesting
## proofy evidence stuff

*Nothing in progression can rest on its original plan.*
*We may as well think of rocking a grown man in the*
*cradle of an infant.*

Edmund Burke

## People get bored

One of the hardest lessons I have learned is how quickly people's interest can be lost.

(Are you still there?)

Jonathan Swift, who wrote *Gulliver's Travels*, was a priest in the Anglican church. In one of his sermons, he quotes from the Book of Acts, chapter 20, verse 9:

"And there sat in a window a certain young man named Eutychus, being fallen into a deep sleep; and as [St] Paul was long preaching, he sunk down with sleep, and fell down from the third loft, and was taken up dead."

Happily, St Paul (being St Paul) was able to bring Eutychus back to life. But since latter-day preachers exceed St Paul in the art of sending people to sleep, Swift says, and since they fall exceedingly short of him in working miracles, modern congregants tend to be more careful about where they station themselves, "for taking their repose without hazard".

If you have ever spoken to a large gathering, you will probably laugh with Swift, and also feel his pain and bewilderment as he describes looking around from the pulpit and observing his flock either asleep or "in a perpetual whisper". It's horrible to be disregarded, whoever you are.

When I got my job as magazine writer, and after I'd written a few – but not many – stories for the magazine, stories that took a good few days to research and write up, I happened to be in a café on a Saturday morning beside a man who had a copy of my magazine in front of him. So exciting!

He had been sitting there for a while, slowly working his way through the main paper and the financial supplement. I was confident that he would come to the magazine eventually because of the way he had carefully placed it beside him, the right way up and ready to open – as opposed to leaving it upside-down on a nearby chair, if you see what I mean.

I got through at least one cup of coffee waiting for him to read it. And eventually the time came.

He was obviously quite a neat chap, and carefully folded the paper so that it looked almost as if it hadn't been read. He slid the magazine out from underneath and put it on top. He ordered another coffee – great news! He was not about to rush off anywhere.

He inspected the contents page carefully, smiled at something, but I have no idea what. Then he slowly read through the short, bitty section at the front, full of wacky novelty and amusement. He read a short interview, all the way to the end. He was coming to the section where the main features could be found! Mine was the second main feature.

He read the first one, but not quite to the end. He was about to read my story!

He turned the page, so that the whole spread was open to him long enough to read the headline, then he turned to the next feature.

At tabloid newspapers, a little before this time, it was not uncommon to find a note pinned to the office wall, reading: "Who the hell reads the second paragraph?" The intention lying behind this rhetorical question was that writers should always contrive to make the first paragraph a knockout. At the *Sun*, in the 1980s, the question was becoming more urgent: "Who the hell reads any of the paragraphs at all?", and editors worked hard to tell readers all they needed to know in the punning, shouty headlines.

In that café, I wondered how many people would read only the headline over my story.

I couldn't bear it. Having skipped my story, the man settled down to read the third feature. I couldn't stay to watch. I was in pain, and conceived an irrational hatred of the writer, whoever it was, of that third feature.

Might it be possible that my non-reader planned to turn back and enjoy my story later? Maybe, but what if he didn't? That would have killed me. I paid for my coffee and left the restaurant, hating not just all the other journalists whose words he did read, but also the innocent non-reader himself, the man who had "ignored me".

I didn't tell anybody. When somebody else, later that weekend, told me they had read my story and enjoyed it, I acted as if I was delighted about the whole thing. Everything was marvellous. But in truth I felt slightly ashamed of my story, because it hadn't proved interesting to this one man, a total stranger, in the moment that I happened to watch him open the page. Not interesting for even three seconds. Wailing and gnashing of teeth hardly begins to describe it.

Only gradually, over a very long period indeed, more than a decade but perhaps not two, did I become microscopically better at handling this kind of disappointment.

I knew it was silly. I knew it wasn't about me being boring (not necessarily, anyway). I knew there were other factors involved: the man in the café might have had a weird phobia about whatever I happened to write about that week (I don't remember what it was), just as my daughter, for a long time, was unable to stay in the room if a shark appeared on TV. I knew that he might possibly have read my story already, or might have planned, when I saw him smiling at the contents page, to save it for a special occasion – perhaps he intended to go home and tell his family that he was cancelling their trip to the opera that evening and he was going to treat them instead to a spoken rendition of an amazing magazine story by a genius called John-Paul Flintoff. Perhaps, indeed.

I knew too that I would never know. But that fearful need to know, that zeal to control the whole universe, is hard to give up. We want people to read and enjoy our writing, laugh at our wedding speeches and hand over oodles of cash to become our customers.

Happily, as Swift and others confirm, I'm not the only one who feels this particular pain. When Brian introduced me to his speechwriters network, I was quietly pleased when one of them told me he gets upset watching the government minister he writes for deliver his carefully chosen words in parliament. Not because the minister does anything wrong, but because the MPs around him, absorbed in their phones, pay no attention.

Today, technology enables newspapers to measure how many (or few) people read which stories online, and for how many seconds or minutes they stay on the page. I know now that my experience was not so bad. My wife works for a major newspaper. Every so often, she tells me how well a particular story has performed, in terms of hits and page-retention, or how badly. High or low, the figures are always salutary, bracing, health-giving: like getting an injection to ward off flu. But it's not flu I'm warding off. It's the sickly neediness of feeling entitled to other people's attention.

I have since had more than a few experiences of speaking in front of people who were happy to show their lack of interest. Before I tell you what happened, I should mention that some years ago I read a book by a man called Keith Johnstone. It was called *Impro*, and it blew my mind. I wondered why I hadn't heard of Johnstone, because it turned out he'd been teaching theatrical improvisation to actors at the Royal Court Theatre in its heyday, in the 1950s and 60s. I read his book several times, scribbling in the margins and underlining and adding comments along the lines of "this is brilliant!" and "amazing!" and "wow!"

Then I discovered that Johnstone was still alive, and still teaching. I signed up for a course, a whole year ahead. It was worth the wait. I learned so much on that course. I booked to do it again, and again, and again. Each time, I learned more. I've subsequently gone on to teach things I learned from Keith, and been delighted to see people's eyes light up as they realised how they could apply improvisation to everyday life. For a time, I was so besotted with improvisation that I turned my back on the thing I have done all my working life – writing stories that are printed, fixed and unchanging.

I see now that this was a mistake: being willing to improvise is a wonderful bonus, best enjoyed by people who prepare and plan.

The reason I mention him here is because Keith gave me the chance, after I'd trained with him for a while, to test people's boredom threshold in a much more direct way, and with more excruciating awkwardness, than by simply watching a stranger read a magazine.

Here's what happened.

By the end of a week together, roughly 25 of us had become OK at improvising. Probably better than OK, but let's settle with OK.

So Keith invited us to try something very simple: go on stage in front of each other and improvise.

Easy! We were trained improvisers. That's what we did.

But he had a twist. "Unlike normal shows, members of the audience have total permission to leave, whenever they lose interest: just get up, quietly, and walk away. No hard feelings. You're helping the performers because you are showing them what works, and what doesn't. Improvisers, if you see people walk away, keep improvising. But when half of the audience has gone, I'm going to stop you, because otherwise there's too much pressure on the people who are still there. Understood?"

To my credit, I had learned by now to trust Keith about not trying to work out a plan before going onstage. Trust in the moment, he said. While waiting for my turn, if my mind started trying to invent things, I stopped, focused on whoever was speaking. "Go up blank," I told myself. "I'll be fine: I'm a storyteller!"

But when people have full permission to leave – well, that changes everything.

As a matter of interest, how long do you think we were able to hold (half) the audience? Remember, we were trained improvisers. We'd trained with Keith Johnstone, the man who wrote the book. We were OK, probably better than OK. How long?

When I tell this story to groups of people, I ask for

suggestions. Often the first person to answer will say, "Twenty minutes?" Then somebody will say, "Twelve minutes." A few more numbers will be called out. Rarely does anybody suggest we could lose our audience in less than five minutes.

In fact, our average time was fifteen seconds. One or two in the group lost half their audience in five seconds, poor souls. Me, I kept going for fifteen seconds – exactly the average. One man, Will, was extraordinary. He kept everybody engaged for a whole 60 seconds – didn't lose anybody – and had to be stopped after that minute with the kind of applause that you might give somebody who had broken the Olympic record for running the marathon (and done it in a spacesuit).

Why am I telling you this? To drive home what you already know: that people can be bored easily.

You might have hoped that you were reading a book that was going to tell you that you can somehow avoid boring anybody, ever. That after finishing the book you would always be utterly fascinating to absolutely everybody. Well, I'm sorry to disappoint. But you didn't really think that, did you?

The purpose of reminding you that people are easily bored is very simple. Those people include you. You get bored sometimes. People should do their best to stop boring you. And you should do your best to stop boring them. And the way to do that is by preparing, knowing your purpose, and arranging your material to best effect, using all that you need and not one speck more.

## Take it apart, to see the workings

Before devising your own next talk or presentation, it will help to look at what somebody else has done, in a speech that was a proven success, then to take it apart carefully and see if you can work out how it was put together.

I've chosen a speech for you to work on. It changed history. I won't tell you, yet, who delivered it, but it was a classic "voice in the wilderness" speech, from somebody desperately trying to get people to stop ignoring a problem and take it seriously.

If you took the basic structure, you could use it to write a speech about a natural disaster, a health crisis, or assorted forms of injustice – almost anything that's unsettling.

I will tell you how I took it apart, and I suggest you do the same as we go along. (Bet you 10p you won't do it. You'll think you can just read it, absorb the essence and skip on. That would be a mistake, but please yourself. If, on the other hand, you do as I suggest – well, I have a shiny 10p coin just for you.)

On a blank sheet of paper, I wrote the topic in the middle. Let's call it "Voice in the Wilderness". Then I drew four branches coming off it, and wrote at the end of each one the following titles: "Intentions", "Credentials", "Reasoning" and "Emotion".

Then I read the speech on paper – first silently in my head, then out loud, then again silently. Only that way could I really get my head around it.

On the third reading, I underlined anything that particularly struck me and added a note about it on my mind map. It's important to emphasise that I didn't do this perfectly.

Not by any means. I made mistakes, put things in what later felt like the wrong place. But that didn't matter. It was the process of doing it that helped me to get my head around the speech. I then re-drew the mind map, not once but twice. And only after that was I able to look at it, breathe deeply and think, yes, that's it.

I'm deliberately not telling you yet what the speech was about, because I'd like to show you the general shape before I fill it with specifics. If I gave you the specifics too soon, you might not see so clearly how you could make your own use of the general shape.

Broadly speaking, speeches tend to move from the past, through the present and into the future. They feature Credentials towards the beginning, Reasoning in the middle, and a nice wodge of Emotion towards the end. But these are broad strokes, not a rule to be followed rigidly. Speaking for myself, I like to kick off with Emotion, getting an audience really engaged, then go back and explain the situation. Sometimes I like to finish with something strictly logical. Each of us has a preference.

If you are just starting and want guidance, stick to the conventional shape.

Now, to a breakdown of the actual speech, with specifics. It was delivered to the House of Commons by Winston Churchill, and you can read the full text below, with footnotes added by me to give a rough sense of how I tried to do the impossible – work out backwards how he put the speech together. You will see (in the footnotes) that I have used the rhetorical terms for Credentials (Ethos), Reasoning (Logos) and Emotion (Pathos).

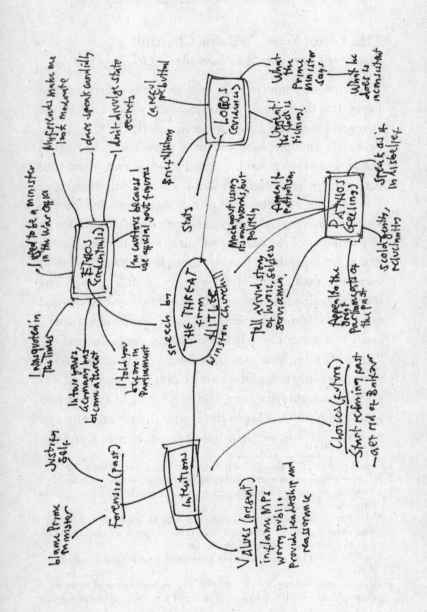

**THE THREAT from HITLER**
*Winston Churchill*

speech by

**ETHOS (credentials)**
- I used to be a minister in the War Office
- My friends make me look moderate
- I dare speak candidly
- I don't divulge state secrets
- I'm cautious because I use special govt figures
- I was quoted in The Times
- In two years, Germany has become a threat
- I told you first in Parliament

**LOGOS (reasons)**
- What the Prime Minister says / What he does is inconsistent
- Urgent! The clock is ticking!
- Brief History
- (Careful) not brutal

**Stats**

**PATHOS (feelings)**
- Appeal to patriotism
- Speak as if in disbelief
- Mock out using their own words, but politely
- Scold gently, No alarmism
- Tell vivid story of heroic, selfless servicemen
- Appeal to the great Parliaments of the past

**Intentions**

**Values (present)**
- inflame MPs
- warn public
- Provide leadership and reassurance

**Choices (future)**
- Start reframing past
- get rid of Baldwin

**Forensic (past)**
- blame Prime Minister
- Justify Self

## "The Locust Years", Winston Churchill
### *House of Commons, 12 November 1936*

I have, with some friends, put an Amendment on the Paper. It is the same as the Amendment which I submitted two years ago,[1] and I have put it in exactly the same terms because I thought it would be a good thing to remind the House of what has happened in these two years. Our Amendment in November 1934 was the culmination of a long series of efforts by private Members and by the Conservative party in the country to warn His Majesty's Government of the dangers to Europe and to this country which were coming upon us through the vast process of German rearmament[2] then already in full swing. The speech which I made on that occasion was much censured as being alarmist[3] by leading Conservative newspapers, and I remember that Mr Lloyd George congratulated the Prime Minister, who was then Lord President, on having so satisfactorily demolished my extravagant fears.

What would have been said,[4] I wonder, if I could two years ago have forecast to the House the actual course of events?[5] Suppose we[6] had then been told that Germany

---

1 *Ethos:* I told you this already. I was right then and I'm right now.

2 *Subject of speech*: rearmament, and Britain's position relative to Germany.

3 *Churchill's argument*: German rearmament is dangerous, and getting more dangerous all the time.

4 *Logos*: Repeat this question, and variations such as "Suppose we had been told" several times, to deliver a stylish, point-by-point rebuttal of the notion that I was ever exaggerating the threat.

5 *Logos*: I was not taken seriously, but I am going to show you exactly how right I was.

6 *Ethos*: To avoid looking like a know-it-all, and retain the sense of common cause with fellow MPs, I shall speak as one of you. We're all in this together!

would spend for two years £800,000,000 a year upon warlike preparations; that her industries would be organised for war, as the industries of no country have ever been; that by breaking all Treaty engagements she would create a gigantic air force and an army based on universal compulsory service, which by the present time, in 1936, amounts to upwards of thirty-nine divisions of highly equipped troops, including mechanised divisions of almost unmeasured strength and that behind all this there lay millions of armed and trained men, for whom the formations and equipment are rapidly being prepared to form another eighty divisions in addition to those already perfected. Suppose we had then known that by now two years of compulsory military service would be the rule, with a preliminary year of training in labour camps; that the Rhineland would be occupied by powerful forces and fortified with great skill, and that Germany would be building with our approval, signified by treaty, a large submarine fleet.

Suppose we had also been able to foresee the degeneration of the foreign situation – our quarrel with Italy, the Italo-German association, the Belgian declaration about neutrality – which, if the worst interpretation of it proves to be true, so greatly affects the security of this country – and the disarray of the smaller Powers of Central Europe. Suppose all that had been forecast – why, no one would have believed in the truth of such a nightmare tale. Yet just two years have gone by and we see it all in broad daylight.[7]

---

7 *Logos:* I have demonstrated the problem, in fine detail.

Where shall we be this time two years? I hesitate now to predict.[8]

Let me say, however, that I will not accept the mood of panic or of despair. There is another side – a side which deserves our study, and can be studied without derogating in any way from the urgency which ought to animate our military preparations. The British Navy is, and will continue to be, incomparably the strongest in Europe. The French Army will certainly be, for a good many months to come, at least equal in numbers and superior in maturity to the German Army. The British and French Air Forces together are a very different proposition from either of those forces considered separately. While no one can prophesy, it seems to me that the Western democracies, provided they are knit closely together, would be tolerably safe for a considerable number of months ahead. No one can say to a month or two, or even a quarter or two, how long this period of comparative equipoise will last. But it seems certain[9] that during the year 1937 the German Army will become more numerous than the French Army, and very much more efficient than it is now. It seems certain that the German Air Force will continue to improve upon the long lead which it already has over us, particularly in respect of long-distance bombing machines. The year 1937 will certainly be marked by a great increase in the adverse

---

8 *Function of speech*: Inform parliament and the general public about the current threat, sow worry and blame the Prime Minister, and persuade MPs to push for immediate and rapid rearmament, according to my prescription.

9 *Logos*: Create an elegantly linked series of alarming, but cautious predictions with the refrain, "it seems certain that...".

factors which only intense efforts on our part can, to effective extent, countervail.

The efforts at rearmament which France and Britain are making will not by themselves be sufficient.[10] It will be necessary for the Western democracies, even at some extension of their risks, to gather round them all the elements of collective security or of combined defensive strength against aggression – if you prefer, as I do myself, to call it so – which can be assembled on the basis of the Covenant of the League of Nations. Thus I hope we may succeed in again achieving a position of superior force, and then will be the time, not to repeat the folly which we committed when we were all-powerful and supreme, but to invite Germany to make common cause with us in assuaging the griefs of Europe and opening a new door to peace and disarmament.

I now turn more directly to the issues of this Debate. Let us examine our own position. No one can refuse his sympathy to the Minister for the Co-ordination of Defence. From time to time my Right Honourable Friend lets fall phrases or facts which show that he realises, more than anyone else on that bench, it seems to me, the danger in which we stand. One such phrase came from his lips the other night. He spoke of "the years that the locust hath eaten".[11] Let us see which are these "years that the locust hath eaten" even if we do not pry too closely in search of the locusts who have eaten these precious years. For this

---

10  *Logos*: Let me bring you up to date on what has happened in the UK and abroad.

11  *Logos*: I'm going to use this rather splendid phrase used only the other day by the minister, and I'm going to bash the government with it.

purpose we must look into the past. From the year 1932, certainly from the beginning of 1933, when Herr Hitler came into power, it was general public knowledge in this country that serious rearmament had begun in Germany. There was a change in the situation. Three years ago, at the Conservative Conference at Birmingham, that vigorous and faithful servant of this country, Lord Lloyd, moved the following resolution:

That this Conference desires to record its grave anxiety in regard to the inadequacy of the provisions made for Imperial Defence.

That was three years ago, and I see, from *The Times* report of that occasion, that I said:[12]

"During the last four or five years the world has grown gravely darker... We have steadily disarmed, partly with a sincere desire to give a lead to other countries, and partly through the severe financial pressure of the time. But a change must now be made. We must not continue longer on a course in which we alone are growing weaker while every other nation is growing stronger."

The resolution was passed unanimously, with only a rider informing the Chancellor of the Exchequer that all necessary burdens of taxation would be cheerfully borne. There were no locusts there, at any rate.

I am very glad to see the Prime Minister [Mr Baldwin] restored to his vigour, and to learn that he has been recuperated by his rest and also, as we hear, rejuvenated.[13] It

---

12 *Ethos:* See, I was quoted in Britain's newspaper of record!
13 *Ethos:* I'm keeping the language very polite.

has been my fortune to have ups and downs in my political relations with him, the downs on the whole predominating perhaps, but at any rate we have always preserved agreeable personal relations, which, so far as I am concerned, are greatly valued. I am sure he would not wish in his conduct of public affairs that there should be any shrinking from putting the real issues of criticism which arise[14], and would certainly proceed in that sense. My Rt Hon Friend has had all the power for a good many years, and therefore there rests upon him inevitably the main responsibility for everything that has been done, or not done, and also the responsibility for what is to be done or not done now. So far as the air is concerned, this responsibility was assumed by him in a very direct personal manner even before he became Prime Minister. I must recall the words which he used in the Debate on 8 March 1934, nearly three years ago. In answer to an appeal which I made to him, both publicly and privately, he said:

"Any Government of this country – a National Government more than any, and this Government – will see to it that in air strength and air power this country shall no longer be in a position inferior to any country within striking distance of our shores."

Well, Sir, I accepted that solemn promise, but some of my friends,[15] like Sir Edward Grigg and Captain Guest,

---

14 *Ethos*: To be clear, I assume that the Prime Minister would prefer me to speak candidly, and I will do so.

15 *Logos, Ethos*: At this point, I'd like to point out that I'm not entirely alone. In fact, my friends have even more extreme views than me, thereby making me seem all the more reasonable.

wanted what the Minister for the Co-ordination of Defence, in another state of being, would have called "further and better particulars", and they raised a debate after dinner, when the Prime Minister, then Lord President, came down to the House and really showed less than his usual urbanity in chiding those Members for even venturing to doubt the intention of the Government to make good in every respect the pledge which he had so solemnly given in the afternoon. I do not think that responsibility was ever more directly assumed in a more personal manner. The Prime Minister was not successful in discharging that task, and he admitted with manly candour[16] a year later that he had been led into error upon the important question of the relative strength of the British and German air power.

No doubt as a whole His Majesty's Government were very slow in accepting the unwelcome fact of German rearmament. They still clung to the policy of one-sided disarmament. It was one of those experiments, we are told, which had to be, to use a vulgarism, "tried out", just as the experiments of non-military sanctions against Italy had to be tried out. Both experiments have now been tried out, and Ministers are accustomed to plume themselves upon the very clear results of those experiments. They are held to prove conclusively that the policies subjected to the experiments were all wrong, utterly foolish, and should never be used again, and the very same men who were foremost in urging those experiments are now foremost in proclaiming

---

16 *Ethos*: I'm so polite you can't quite tell if I'm making fun of the Prime Minister here.

and denouncing the fallacies upon which they were based. They have bought their knowledge, they have bought it dear,[17] they have bought it at our expense, but at any rate let us be duly thankful that they now at last possess it.

In July 1935, before the General Election, there was a very strong movement in this House in favour of the appointment of a Minister to concert the action of the three fighting Services. Moreover, at that time the Departments of State were all engaged in drawing up the large schemes of rearmament in all branches which have been laid before us in the White Paper and upon which we are now engaged. One would have thought that that was the time when this new Minister or Co-ordinator was most necessary. He was not, however, in fact appointed until nearly nine months later, in March 1936. No explanation has yet been given to us why these nine months were wasted[18] before the taking of what is now an admittedly necessary measure. The Prime Minister dilated the other night, no doubt very properly, the great advantages which had flowed from the appointment of the Minister for the Co-ordination of Defence. Every argument used to show how useful has been the work which he has done accuses the failure to appoint him nine months earlier, when inestimable benefits would have accrued to us by the saving of this long period.

When at last, in March, after all the delays, the Prime

---

17 *Logos:* The government made mistakes, and learned from them, but too slowly and at a high price to us all.

18 *Logos*: The government says it will do something, but doesn't do it – and won't explain why.

Minister eventually made the appointment, the arrangement of duties was so ill-conceived that no man could possibly discharge them with efficiency or even make a speech about them without embarrassment. I have repeatedly pointed out the obvious mistake in organisation of jumbling together – and practically everyone in the House is agreed upon this – the functions of defence with those of a Minister of Supply. The proper organisation, let me repeat, is four Departments – the Navy, the Army, the Air and the Ministry of Supply, with the Minister for the Co-ordination of Defence over the four, exercising a general supervision, concerting their actions, and assigning the high priorities of manufacture in relation to some comprehensive strategic conception. The House is familiar with the many requests and arguments which have been made to the Government to create a Ministry of Supply. These arguments have received powerful reinforcement from another angle in the report of the Royal Commission on Arms Manufacture. The first work of this new Parliament, and the first work of the Minister for the Co-ordination of Defence if he had known as much about the subject when he was appointed as he does now, would have been to set up a Ministry of Supply which should, step by step, have taken over the whole business of the design and manufacture of all the supplies needed by the Air Force and the Army, and everything needed for the Navy, except warships, heavy ordnance, torpedoes and one or two ancillaries. All the best of the industries of Britain should have been surveyed from a general integral standpoint, and all existing resources utilised so far as was necessary to execute the programme.

The Minister for the Co-ordination of Defence has argued as usual against a Ministry of Supply. The arguments which he used were weighty, and even ponderous – it would disturb and delay existing programmes; it would do more harm than good; it would upset the life and industry of the country; it would destroy the export trade and demoralise finance at the moment when it was most needed; it would turn this country into one vast munitions camp. Certainly these are massive arguments, if they are true. One would have thought that they would carry conviction to any man who accepted them. But then my Rt Hon Friend went on somewhat surprisingly to say, "The decision is not final". It would be reviewed again in a few weeks. What will you know in a few weeks about this matter that you do not know now,[19] that you ought not to have known a year ago, and have not been told any time in the last six months? What is going to happen in the next few weeks which will invalidate all these magnificent arguments by which you have been overwhelmed, and suddenly make it worth your while to paralyse the export trade, to destroy the finances, and to turn the country into a great munitions camp?

The First Lord of the Admiralty in his speech the other night went even farther. He said, "We are always reviewing the position." Everything, he assured us, is entirely fluid. I am sure that that is true. Anyone can see what the position

---

19 *Logos*: I'm going to shoot you down with my machine-gun of rhetorical questions.

is. The Government simply cannot make up their minds, or they cannot get the Prime Minister to make up his mind.[20] So they go on in strange paradox, decided only to be undecided, resolved to be irresolute, adamant for drift, solid for fluidity, all-powerful to be impotent. So we go on preparing more months and years – precious, perhaps vital to the greatness of Britain – for the locusts to eat. They will say to me, "A Minister of Supply is not necessary, for all is going well." I deny it. "The position is satisfactory." It is not true. "All is proceeding according to plan." We know what that means.

Let me come to the Territorial Army. In March of this year I stigmatised a sentence in the War Office Memorandum about the Territorial Army, in which it was said the equipment of the Territorials could not be undertaken until that of the Regular Army had been completed. What has been done about all that?

It is certain the evils are not yet removed. I agree wholeheartedly with all that was said by Lord Winterton the other day about the Army and the Territorial Force. When I think how these young men who join the Territorials come forward, almost alone in the population, and take on a liability to serve anywhere in any part of the world, not even with a guarantee to serve in their own units; come forward in spite of every conceivable deterrent; come forward – 140,000 of them, although they are still not up to strength – and then find that the Government does not

---

20 *Logos*: Watch this! I'm going to laugh at the government's indecisions with a witty statement in five paradoxes.

take their effort seriously enough even to equip and arm them properly,[21] I marvel at their patriotism. It is a marvel; it is also a glory, but a glory we have no right to profit by unless we can secure proper and efficient equipment for them.

A friend of mine the other day saw a number of persons engaged in peculiar evolutions, genuflections and gestures in the neighbourhood of London. His curiosity was excited.[22] He wondered whether it was some novel form of gymnastics, or a new religion – there are new religions which are very popular in some countries nowadays – or whether they were a party of lunatics out for an airing. On approaching closer he learned that they were a Searchlight Company of London Territorials who were doing their exercises as well as they could without having the searchlights. Yet we are told there is no need for a Ministry of Supply.

In the manoeuvres of the Regular Army many of the most important new weapons have to be represented by flags and discs. When we remember how small our land forces are – altogether only a few hundred thousand men – it seems incredible that the very flexible industry of Britain, if properly handled, could not supply them with their modest requirements. In Italy, whose industry is so much smaller, whose wealth and credit are a small fraction of this country's, a Dictator is able to boast that he

---

21  *Logos*: In passing, I shall now lob the suggestion that the Prime Minister is himself the greatest threat to his armed forces, an unexploded grenade in the middle of my sentence.

22  *Pathos, Logos*: A vivid story to engage the audience with the plight of actual servicemen struggling to do their best without equipment. This vivid paragraph captures the purpose of the whole speech.

has bayonets and equipment for 8,000,000 men. Halve the figure, if you like, and the moral remains equally cogent. The Army lacks almost every weapon which is required for the latest form of modern war. Where are the anti-tank guns, where are the short-distance wireless sets, where the field anti-aircraft guns against low-flying armoured aeroplanes? We want to know how it is that this country, with its enormous motoring and motor-bicycling public, is not able to have strong mechanised divisions, both Regular and Territorial. Surely, when so much of the interest and the taste of our youth is moving in those mechanical channels, and when the horse is receding with the days of chivalry into the past, it ought to be possible to create an army of the size we want fully up to strength and mechanised to the highest degree.

Look at the Tank Corps. The tank was a British invention.[23] This idea, which has revolutionised the conditions of modern war, was a British idea forced on the War Office by outsiders. Let me say they would have just as hard work today to force a new idea on it. I speak from what I know.[24] During the War we had almost a monopoly, let alone the leadership, in tank warfare, and for several years afterwards we held the foremost place. To England all eyes were turned. All that has gone now. Nothing has been done in "the years that the locust hath eaten" to equip the Tank Corps with new machines. The medium tank which they possess, which in its day was the best in the world, is

---

23  *Pathos*: Appeal to patriotism to sting MPs into action.
24  *Ethos*: I was a minister at the War Office during the Great War, so I know what I'm talking about.

now looking obsolete. Not only in numbers – for there we have never tried to compete with other countries – but in quality these British weapons are now surpassed by those of Germany, Russia, Italy and the United States. All the shell plants and gun plants in the Army, apart from the very small peace-time services, are in an elementary stage. A very long period must intervene before any effectual flow of munitions can be expected, even for the small forces of which we dispose. Still we are told there is no necessity for a Ministry of Supply, no emergency which should induce us to impinge on the normal course of trade. If we go on like this, and I do not see what power can prevent us from going on like this, some day there may be a terrible reckoning, and those who take the responsibility so entirely upon themselves are either of a hardy disposition or they are incapable of foreseeing the possibilities which may arise.[25]

Now I come to the greatest matter of all, the air. We received on Tuesday night, from the First Lord of the Admiralty, the assurance that there is no foundation whatever for the statement that we are "vastly behind hand" with our Air Force programme. It is clear from his words that we are behind hand. The only question is, what meaning does the First Lord attach to the word "vastly"? He also used the expression, about the progress of air expansion, that it was "not unsatisfactory". One does not know what his standard is. His standards change from time to time.[26]

---

25 *Logos*: Dire prediction that obliquely calls the government either reckless or blind.

26 *Logos*: I don't know about you, but I get the sense that the government isn't being straight, or doesn't know what it's doing.

In that speech of the 11th of September about the League of Nations there was one standard, and in the Hoare-Laval Pact there was clearly another. In August last some of us went in a deputation to the Prime Minister in order to express the anxieties which we felt about national defence, and to make a number of statements which we preferred not to be forced to make in public. I personally made a statement on the state of the Air Force to the preparation of which I had devoted several weeks and which, I am sorry to say, took an hour to read. My Rt Hon Friend the Prime Minister listened with his customary exemplary patience. I think I told him beforehand that he is a good listener, and perhaps he will retort that he learned to be when I was his colleague. At any rate, he listened with patience, and that is always something. During the three months that have passed since then I have checked those facts again in the light of current events and later acknowledge, and were it not that foreign ears listen to all that is said here, or if we were in secret Session,[27] I would repeat my statement here. And even if only one half were true I am sure the House would consider that a very grave state of emergency existed, and also, I regret to say, a state of things from which a certain suspicion of mismanagement cannot be excluded.[28] I am not going into any of those details. I make it a rule, as far as I possibly can, to say nothing in this House upon

---

27 *Ethos*: I am a responsible politician and wouldn't dream of divulging state secrets in my speech.

28 *Logos*: Understatement keeps me looking reasonable. "Mismanagement cannot be excluded" isn't quite the same as saying "the government messed up", but it's close.

matters which I am not sure are already known to the General Staffs of foreign countries; but there is one statement of very great importance which the Minister for the Co-ordination of Defence made in his speech on Tuesday. He said:

"The process of building up squadrons and forming new training units and skeleton squadrons is familiar to everybody connected with the Air Force. The number of squadrons in present circumstances at home today is eighty, and that figure includes sixteen auxiliary squadrons, but excludes the Fleet Air Arm, and, of course, does not include the squadrons abroad."

From that figure, and the reservations by which it was prefaced, it is possible for the House, and also for foreign countries, to deduce pretty accurately the progress of our Air Force expansion. I feel, therefore, at liberty to comment on it.

Parliament was promised a total of seventy-one new squadrons, making a total of 124 squadrons in the home defence force, by 31 March 1937. This was thought to be the minimum compatible with our safety. At the end of the last financial year our strength was fifty-three squadrons, including auxiliary squadrons. Therefore, in the thirty-two weeks which have passed since the financial year began we have added twenty-eight squadrons – that is to say, less than one new squadron each week. In order to make the progress which Parliament was promised, in order to maintain the programme which was put forward as the minimum, we shall have to add forty-three squadrons in the remaining twenty weeks, or over two squadrons a week. The rate at which new squadrons will have to be formed from now till the end of March will have to be nearly three times as fast as hitherto. I do not propose to analyse the composition of the eighty squadrons we now have, but the Minister, in his speech, used a suggestive expression, "skeleton squadrons", applying at least to a portion of them but even if every one of the eighty squadrons had an average strength of twelve aeroplanes, each fitted with war equipment, and the reserves upon which my Rt Hon Friend dwelt, we should only have a total of 960 first-line home-defence aircraft.

What is the comparable German strength? I am not going to give an estimate and say that the Germans have not got more than a certain number, but I will take it upon myself to say that they most certainly at this moment have not got less than a certain number. Most certainly they have not got less than 1,500 first-line aeroplanes, comprised in not less than 130 or 140 squadrons, including auxiliary squadrons. It must also be remembered that Germany has not got in its squadrons any machine the design and construction of which is more than three years old. It must also be remembered that Germany has specialised in long-distance bombing aeroplanes and that her preponderance in that respect is far greater than any of these figures would suggest.[29]

We were promised most solemnly by the Government that air parity with Germany would be maintained by the home-defence forces. At the present time, putting

---

29 *Ethos*: Understatement gives me credibility.

everything at the very best, we are, upon the figures given by the Minister for the Co-ordination of Defence, only about two-thirds as strong as the German Air Force, assuming that I am not very much understating their present strength. How then does the First Lord of the Admiralty [Sir Samuel Hoare] think it right to say:

"On the whole, our forecast of the strength of other Air Forces proves to be accurate; on the other hand, our own estimates have also proved to be accurate. I am authorised to say that the position is satisfactory."

I simply cannot understand it. Perhaps the Prime Minister will explain the position. I should like to remind the House that I have made no revelation affecting this country and that I have introduced no new fact in our air defence which does not arise from the figures given by the Minister and from the official estimates that have been published.[30]

What ought we to do? I know of only one way in which this matter can be carried further. The House ought to demand a Parliamentary inquiry. It ought to appoint six, seven or eight independent Members, responsible, experienced, discreet Members, who have some acquaintance with these matters and are representative of all parties, to interview Ministers and to find out what are, in fact, the answers to a series of questions; then to make a brief report to the House, whether of reassurance or of suggestion for remedying the shortcomings. That, I think,

---

30 *Ethos*: I am careful and scrupulous and rely only on official figures from the government itself.

is what any Parliament worthy of the name would do in these circumstances. Parliaments of the past days in which the greatness of our country was abuilding would never have hesitated.[31] They would have felt they could not discharge their duty to their constituents if they did not satisfy themselves that the safety of the country was being effectively maintained.

The French Parliament, through its committees, has a very wide, deep knowledge of the state of national defence, and I am not aware that their secrets leak out in any exceptional way. There is no reason why our secrets should leak out in any exceptional way. It is because so many members of the French Parliament are associated in one way or another with the progress of the national defence that the French Government were induced to supply, six years ago, upward of £60,000,000 sterling to construct the Maginot Line of fortifications, when our Government was assuring them that wars were over and that France must not lag behind Britain in her disarmament. Even now I hope that Members of the House of Commons will rise above considerations of party discipline, and will insist upon knowing where we stand in a matter which affects our liberties and our lives. I should have thought that the Government, and above all the Prime Minister, whose load is so heavy, would have welcomed such a suggestion.

Owing to past neglect, in the face of the plainest

---

31  *Pathos*: I call on the patriotic memory of the great parliaments of the past to shame this one into action.

warnings, we have now entered upon a period of danger greater than has befallen Britain since the U-boat campaign was crushed; perhaps, indeed, it is a more grievous period than that, because at that time at least we were possessed of the means of securing ourselves and of defeating that campaign. Now we have no such assurance. The era of procrastination, of half-measures, of soothing and baffling expedients, of delays, is coming to its close. In its place we are entering a period of consequences. We have entered a period in which for more than a year, or a year and a half, the considerable preparations which are now on foot in Britain will not, as the Minister clearly showed, yield results which can be effective in actual fighting strength; while during this very period Germany may well reach the culminating point of her gigantic military preparations, and be forced by financial and economic stringency to contemplate a sharp decline, or perhaps some other exit from her difficulties. It is this lamentable conjunction of events which seems to present the danger of Europe in its most disquieting form. We cannot avoid this period; we are in it now. Surely, if we can abridge it by even a few months, if we can shorten this period when the German Army will begin to be so much larger than the French Army, and before the British Air Force has come to play its complementary part, we may be the architects who build the peace of the world on sure foundations.

Two things, I confess, have staggered me,[32] after a long

---

32 *Pathos*: I really can't believe it. That it should come to this!

Parliamentary experience, in these Debates. The first has been the dangers that have so swiftly come upon us in a few years, and have been transforming our position and the whole outlook of the world. Secondly, I have been staggered by the failure of the House of Commons to react effectively against those dangers. That, I am bound to say, I never expected. I never would have believed that we should have been allowed to go on getting into this plight, month by month and year by year, and that even the Government's own confessions of error would have produced no concentration of Parliamentary opinion and force[33] capable of lifting our efforts to the level of emergency. I say that unless the House resolves to find out the truth for itself it will have committed an act of abdication of duty without parallel in its long history.

---

33 *Pathos*: Parliamentarians, you should be ashamed of yourselves. Are you not worried yet?

## Reading the room: remember the Who

Thinking back on what we covered in the previous chapter, I asked myself what Churchill hoped to achieve with this speech. He states explicitly that he wants parliament to push for rearmament, but was there more? Were there subsidiary aims that might help him to achieve that? To find them, I considered his (mixed) audience. This included: the Prime Minister, Stanley Baldwin; the cabinet generally; Churchill's fellow MPs (his own party and the other parties); the people who elected Churchill to parliament; newspaper reporters, their editors and proprietors; the general public; and foreign governments (allies and enemies).

These different audiences could always be broken down further, but even this overview makes it clear that they had very different needs, hopes and fears. The more I contemplated the conflicting interests, the dizzier I became. Plainly, Britain's allies would welcome an increase in British military strength, while her enemies would not. But what about the cabinet? Did they like having their leader Baldwin mocked by Churchill? Some may have wanted to get rid of Baldwin, others probably didn't. Newspapers would also take a variety of positions. Churchill's voters might either have applauded him or thought he was destabilising the government they helped to elect.

It's important to understand that the Churchill who gave this speech was not the man who has since been identified as the Greatest Briton of all time. As he makes clear in the speech itself, he had been pressing this case for a long time, with scant success. He was getting a reputation for dealing in prophecies of doom, and might reasonably have felt that the more he pressed his point, the less people would pay attention.

I highlight this point because I'm aware that you might be thinking this has nothing to do with you. You're not a politician. So let me tell you briefly about a lawyer I know. She's not the kind of lawyer who works in court, and public speaking isn't her idea of fun.

Several times in her career, she told me, she's been invited ("aka obliged", she says) to address big client events or events where the audience is made up of other lawyers ("even more scary"). As well as the inevitable nerves, she says she feels utterly terrified that somebody will try to catch her out, humiliate her by pointing out factual errors or hideously, laughably wrong interpretation.

Well, Churchill never stopped fearing the same thing. You might say that he chose to be an MP, so he was asking for it; likewise my lawyer friend chose to be a lawyer, and knew that occasional speaking would be required. You might say that Churchill wasn't invited ("aka obliged") to give this particular speech – but given how high the stakes were, he must have felt that there was little choice.

We all feel, occasionally, as if we have no choice – but we do have a choice. And when we feel ready to seize it, we're ready to do it well.

Now, where was I?

Ah, yes, working out backwards how Churchill prepared. He will have known, as we all learn eventually, that it is hard to persuade anybody to change their mind about any topic, if they have strongly aligned themselves to a particular position. And that was the case for all parliamentarians, on this particular issue – the Prime Minister more than any other – because to change your mind can be seen as weakness and loss of face.

For both these reasons, it would help Churchill to bring in new information, which he does. This could remove any lingering sense that he was drearily obsessed; and give grounds for others to shift their position.

Mind you, Churchill was not looking to save everybody from embarrassment. An argument is strengthened by the real sense of the alternative. To make his own policy and determination obvious, Churchill set against it the failed policy and indecision of the Prime Minister and the cabinet.

He deliberately set out to hurt the reputation of the government, so that parliament might step in to demand action. He was rallying his peers to topple the people in charge – just as shareholders might do at the AGM of a badly managed company. (But of course he used polite language, suitable to parliamentary proceedings.)

Remember what I said back in Chapter 1 about speeches needing an adversary? To be clear: I don't mean adversary in the usual sense. I mean, "the holder of ideas contrary to the ideas you are trying to get across". In Churchill's speech, his subject was the threat from Nazi Germany, but rhetorically his "adversary" (in the sense I am using it here) was the indecisive British government. In Henry V's Crispin speech, the real-world enemy was the French army, massively outnumbering the English, but the rhetorical adversary was an English nobleman who expressed regret that there were so few English soldiers: Henry sets out to prove him wrong, to show that the fewer men there are, the greater the share of honour. That nobleman's handwringing is a gift to Henry, because it gives him a rhetorical adversary.

Another thing to consider, in assessing the aims of a speech, is to look for clues in how it handles the past, present and future.

In general, talking about the past is where a speaker assigns praise and blame. This is called forensic rhetoric, and accounts for a great deal of what is spoken in criminal courts, for obvious reasons. Thus, when speakers talk about the past, they are in effect adopting the role of lawyer (either for the prosecution or the defence). Churchill is always polite and careful not to brag, but you can't fail to understand that he is saying: 1. I was right all along, what I predicted has come true and in fact it's even worse than that, and 2. The Prime Minister has been mistaken, is obstinate and remains laughably indecisive, or it would be laughable if the situation wasn't so grave.

Talking about the present is known as demonstrative rhetoric. It's how we set out our values, our beliefs and what we have in common. We do this by stating positives, but we also define ourselves by negatives – the things we don't believe, do or possess in common. We define ourselves by the people we let in, and by the others we keep out. By stating any particular affiliation, Churchill could be said also to be hinting at what he is against. If forensic rhetoric is for lawyers, demonstrative rhetoric is the domain of preachers. The value that the Reverend Churchill wishes to promote more than any other, in this speech, is resolve, driven by a clear statement of urgency and importance.

Talking about the future involves making choices. This is known as deliberative rhetoric. Churchill intends, having set out a clear picture of the past and the present, to make the best possible case for immediate and rapid rearmament.

That, anyway, was my best guess, based on the speech itself and the vague, possibly confused sense of World War II history that is a kind of birthright for people of my age and nationality. I may be wrong, I often am, in more ways than could possibly be imagined. This is just my take on the speech. If you have read the speech, and taken notes, you will have your own. (And you can have my shiny 10p.)

Let's go back to look at how Churchill handles Credentials (which Greek rhetoric called Ethos), Reasoning (Logos) and Emotion (Pathos).

Churchill starts by making clear that he is somebody who has been urging rearmament for some time. In the course of his speech he mentions having attempted to persuade parliament two years previously, quotes himself in *The Times* newspaper, reminds listeners that he worked in the War Office during the previous war and mentions a private meeting with the Prime Minister in which he set out his case for a whole hour. Taken in turn, these points respectively allow Churchill to present himself as a far-sighted prophet, taken seriously by Britain's newspaper of record, a man of deep and relevant experience in office and someone who deserves (and gets) a lengthy audience with the leader of the government.

Looking back, knowing what we know, it might seem that Churchill is overdoing it on his Credentials (Ethos). Did he really need to point these things out? Didn't his record stand for itself? The answer is no. His reputation at this time was not great, and he clearly felt it necessary to talk himself up, albeit in a roundabout and unshowy way. Later, when he was prime minister, he had no need to justify himself – he was prime minister!

Next: his statement of facts and general Reasoning (Logos). What has happened, what circumstances do we find ourselves in, what are the options, what objections will be made? Churchill goes back two years and brings his listeners up to date. As he does this, he slowly and carefully shows that the government wasted nine months getting round to doing what it promised to do. Using the government's own figures, he demonstrates that Germany poses a real threat, and that the threat is growing every month. He uses quotes from the Prime Minister and other ministers to demonstrate their indecision, failing to explain themselves and even chiding those who, like Churchill himself, dared to express doubts.

Towards the end of the speech, Churchill brings in his emotional appeal (Pathos). He holds up the admirable example of young men who have come forward to serve in the armed forces, vividly describing them exercising without the necessary equipment – a story that encapsulates the whole point of his speech. He appeals to patriotism, by showing that Britain, despite having invented the tank, now has fewer of them, and of lower quality, than friends and enemies alike. He appeals to history, to the great parliaments of the past that made Britain great, and obliquely rebukes his contemporaries for allowing the country to find itself in its present position.

## Call to action

Henry V's call to action could be summarised thus: "Chaps, get your swords out and follow me." Churchill's might be: "Dear MPs, help me to light a fire under the backside of the Prime Minister."

One of the hardest calls to action, if not as hard as getting an army excited about going into battle, is to induce an audience to part with its money. Someone who knows all about that is Fred Mulder, a British-Canadian philanthropist, who set up an event that turned into a series of events, then spread to several other countries, all the time raising money for good causes. It's called The Funding Network.

As a successful art dealer, Mulder had frequently funded good causes himself, but found it oddly unsatisfying. Most fundraising events only promote a single cause. Mulder wanted to offer more: "I wanted something more like a marketplace, so that people could listen to a variety of presentations," he told me, sitting in his garden one evening. "I thought, you never go into a shop and only see one pair of trousers."

Another problem with fundraising events, he said, was that if you didn't give money straight away, you might be given a form to take home. "And my experience was, I would take the form home, it would gradually get buried and in the end I would throw it away."

Also, he never knew quite how much to give.

His solution was something more like the auctions he attended as an art collector. "I wanted something that was live, so you had to make a decision at the time, and I wanted to hear what other people were giving."

The Funding Network brings together philanthropists with lots of money and others with only a little. Representatives of the chosen causes give a talk for six minutes, then answer questions for six minutes. At the end, the presenters leave the room and a host conducts a pledging session – a kind of auction for philanthropy. "But we're not competing, like art dealers. If we're competing against anything, it's against apathy."

Since it was set up, The Funding Network has raised nearly £12m. Not a lot by some standards, but not bad considering that most of the donations are less than £100, often much less. It's worth making clear exactly how attractive this must be to good causes wondering where to get some funding: The Funding Network brings together people who have come precisely in order to give money. There's no need for even the most timid presenter to feel awkward asking for cash, because attendees can give as much or as little as they like, and the presenter will never know who gave what.

And yet, even here there is awkwardness. Because every presenter knows that they may be given less cash than other causes, on the night, and less than they had hoped for. As ever, the difference between going home with a bounce in your stride or a foot-dragging crawl is the quality of your presentation.

To find out more, I asked Mulder if I could attend one of The Funding Network's training sessions.

There were four would-be presenters, all women, sitting around a conference room table in a grand office lent by one of the charity's corporate supporters. The women would be pitching in just two weeks, and with little preamble, the charity's events manager Jennie Jeffery got the meeting going by asking them to introduce themselves in just 60 seconds. The first managed to do this in 40 seconds. The next two overran. The last took 90 seconds. Jeffery was relaxed about these minor crimes, but noted firmly that they would not be able to overrun in the real session.

If there's more than you can say, she added, mention it during the six-minute Q&A after your pitch.

She handed out a pre-printed sheet, indicating six "pitch-building blocks", with space beneath each of the following headers for individuals to fill out their own story.

- Introduce yourself and your organisation. Your motivation, your purpose (60 secs)
- The problem. Key statistic, real-life example (60 secs)
- Your solution. What you do. How it works. Why your organisation? (120 secs)
- Your impact. Evidence to date, what you plan next (60 secs)
- Case Study. Example of success. Emphasise the human aspect (60 secs)
- Call to action. Financial ask? Non-financial ask? (30 secs)

I stared at the paper for a moment, in wonder: this guide could help participants to raise £6,000 in six minutes, or 12 minutes if you include Q&A. To put it another way: it was a recipe for earning £500 a minute. Quite a valuable piece of paper! Mind you, this kind of guidance can be found all over the internet. It's not complicated. It's obvious. It's common sense. But people still need it. Until they know better, people make stupid mistakes, and this could help them!

I seized control of my wandering thoughts and gave my attention to events in the room.

Holding up the pre-printed sheet, Jeffery stressed that it was not prescriptive, just a guide. Then the women took turns to practise their pitches more fully, and afterwards Jeffery gave feedback to them all. The following summaries are brisker than she was in person. The first pitch was a bit "high level", she said, a bit abstract. "Tell stories. Make it human. Make it personal." With another, she praised the way the presenter brought in a recent national news story, making her cause highly relevant. "But can you give a sense of the scale of the problem?" The woman who overran at the beginning of the training session had overrun again, and still not finished before Jeffery cut her off. "Don't dwell too long on the problem," Jeffery said. "Maybe one minute. Make it clear that this is a huge issue, and you can't capture it all now. Just pick a couple of key elements. The hardest thing is deciding what to leave out. Perhaps you could practise with people who don't know much about it? Focus on the solution. The solution is the main part, and should be exciting."

There was something else that troubled me about the last woman's pitch.

## Unanswered questions

The woman's subject was dolls for young girls. Her argument was that girls in Africa have to make do with dolls that are pale skinned, or dolls that recall racist stereotypes, and that they should be provided with dolls that look like themselves. Her purpose was to raise money to develop this concept.

So far as this goes, I'm with her. But my mind was wandering again. I kept thinking: Yep, this is not good, but why are you telling us this? Because, you see, the speaker was white.

I don't want to get into the rights and wrongs of white people speaking up for black people. I really don't, and I won't. All I want is to tell you what was happening in my head. I may be odd – in fact, I have no doubt about that – but I am a human being, one of just five human beings in her audience at that moment, and my mind was racing. I strongly suspect that I wasn't the only person troubled by this unanswered question. And the longer she kept it unanswered, the more difficult I found it to attend to her otherwise very interesting and motivating insights. My curious mind was going: "Yeah but yeah but yeah but you haven't told us..."

And the reason I mention these uncontrollable mental shenanigans is simple: your audience will have lots of questions too. A good part of arranging your talk involves predicting what those questions will be, and answering them at the right time.

This applies to every type of work that unfolds through time. Behind me, builders have been putting together a block of flats for the last two years. They're approaching completion now, and I have a clearer sense of why they did what they did in the sequence they chose. But for months I've been walking up to my office with cups of coffee and stopping at the window and asking myself: Why are they doing that now? Why didn't they do this first, or that? When will they do the other thing (whatever it is) that I know they're planning? When will they stop making such a racket, with the beeps of the vehicles driving backwards, intermittent drilling into bricks, low-level churn from a cement mixer and syncopated grinding from the chap slicing slabs of concrete pavement? How am I supposed to write this book with all that going on?

As this suggests, I have largely been an unwilling spectator, but despite myself I have also been curious, and at times (I confess) even sometimes admired the elegant resolution of my questions.

Your audience may be like me. Or they may be more generous, like the big-hearted people who come to events at The Funding Network. But whoever they are, they will have some kind of brain, and the assembled brains before you will be fizzing with questions as you unfold your ideas. Your job is to guess what those questions are.

## Dance of the seven veils

Despite all you read in the last paragraphs, sometimes it's necessary, or just more fun, to keep the audience waiting.

There are good reasons for both. Right now, I'll bet you have a few questions of your own. You're thinking: OK, Flintoff, but you still haven't told me about X!

To which I can only reply that I'm not a mind-reader, and can't possibly predict the questions that will be running through the head of everybody who ever reads this, far less you, the very special individual who is reading this particular sentence right now (yes, I only care about you, just you, because you're so very, very special, the rest can go jump in a lake). I'm not a mind-reader, but I do have a few ideas regarding what you might want to know more about. I have my suspicions. For instance, I'm pretty confident that you have flicked through the book a bit already, and jumped ahead to peek for answers in the tantalising sections still ahead of us. You're a cheeky monkey! But I like you, and I'm glad you're still here. Go ahead, take a peek, I don't mind. Make yourself at home.

I have some idea what you might be thinking about because I deliberately left some threads hanging. And I think that you know that I did that, here and there. It's a tease, like the dance of the seven veils. I've never actually watched a dance of the seven veils, to be honest, but I understand the principle, and I imagine that it's more successful if viewers don't know there are seven. Take off the first one, and they're surprised to see another underneath. Take that one off, and the third will be a shock, perhaps a disappointment. By the fifth, they're frustrated but also titillated; and by the time you get to the seventh veil – well, gosh, they're beside themselves.

Good storytellers use this approach deliberately, and with experience they learn to avoid raising questions that are merely distracting. I'm still learning, so please forgive me if there's something I've missed. It may help you to forgive me if I tell you about something that happened at the headquarters of Amazon, the world's biggest online retailer.

In 2012, the company's founder Jeff Bezos announced that he had abandoned the use of PowerPoint slides. Staff meetings would begin instead with 30 minutes of silent reading. He explained: "The traditional corporate meeting starts with a presentation. Somebody gets up in front of the room and presents, with PowerPoint, some type of slide show."

(PowerPoint, if you don't know, perhaps because you are a newborn innocent, or because you picked up a copy of this book on another planet, many years in the future, is a digital version of the photographic slides that were used in the 20th century to illustrate talks. PowerPoint slides, gathered into virtual "decks", are easy to produce and fill with text, and their use spread like a contagious disease in the late 20th and early 21st century.)

"In our view, you get very little information on slides," said Bezos. "You get bullet points. This is easy for the presenter, but difficult for the audience. And so instead all of our meetings are structured around a six-page narrative memo. When you have to write your ideas out in complete sentences, complete paragraphs, it forces deeper clarity."

Asked why not read the memos before the meeting, he said: "Time does not come from nowhere. This way, you know everyone has the time to read. The author gets the nice warm feeling of seeing their hard work being read. If you have a PowerPoint presentation, executives interrupt. If you have a six-page memo, on page two you have a question but on page four that question is answered."

What has this to do with my dance of the seven veils? I hope that if you found a question on page two, you found the answer on page four, as it were. If not, perhaps you will find it on the pages ahead. More importantly, what happened at Amazon might give you an idea about what you could include in a briefing note for your own audience.

## Cliffhangers, or loose ends

The question of what to reveal, and when, is fundamentally an artistic question. As with so much else, it will help you to find your answer if you consider the purpose of your communication.

If you are raising money to manufacture ethnically various dolls, you want to encourage your audience to believe not only that they should give you money but that they should give you lots of it. I'm sure you can imagine that there may be some barriers in the way of this happy eventuality. What are the barriers, and how can you help your audience to pull them down?

Start by looking for clues within yourself. What causes you, instead of somebody else, to be here, asking for that money? Why aren't you instead (say) sitting in the cinema, or eating an ice cream on your sunny terrace or watching your football team lose (again)? Whatever led you, inexorably, to care so much about this doll situation provides a clue to the barriers that you yourself pulled down.

But when you think how to present this "backstory", don't make the mistake of revealing the outcome all at once. That would be Very Boring Indeed. Stories unfold gradually, and only in that unfolding do they allow the storyteller to drop facts, timelines, laws, precedents and statistics – the things classical orators tell you to put into a good speech. It's certainly possible to deliver facts, timelines, laws, precedents and statistics without stories, but it's also likely to be Very Boring Indeed.

Whether you are informing, persuading or inspiring, you must be entertaining. Not funny, necessarily. You can be entertaining with a story that is tragic and brings your listeners to tears.

I'll tell you how, but first I must give you a quick history of preaching in Western Europe.

(Note: that last paragraph was a flagrant cliffhanger. I wrote it so that you would roll your eyes and mutter, "Oh, bother!" (or similar). I wrote it so that you would see that by promising to deliver something exciting and valuable shortly, I buy myself time to deliver information that you might otherwise expect to be boring. This is what every TV drama does: "Tune in tomorrow to find out if she divorces him!" And when you start watching the next day, the programme makers string you along for what feels like an eternity of supposedly comic exchanges in the sweet shop, tedious dialogue about pensions, or whatever. It's the old dance-of-the-seven-veils routine.

As I mentioned earlier, I learned very quickly when writing for magazines that people get bored, and that there are various routines that might buy me time while keeping the reader's interest, and these apply to speaking too. One of the greatest lessons I learned was from an article that has taken on almost legendary status in my mind, in the years since I read it. It was about freediving, the sport of daredevils who dive to great depths without breathing equipment. Fairly near the beginning, the journalist asked a tantalising question about how long I, the reader, could hold my breath. I think (but I'm not certain, I may be making this up) that the average person could hold their breath for as long as it took to boil a kettle, walk up five flights of stairs, dead-head 25 roses, or whatever. And he promised to reveal the much greater length of time that the particular diver he was writing about could hold his breath. Then the writer got stuck into telling his story, taking us under the water with his diver, dropping the odd fact, timeline, law, precedent, statistic along the way. It was so absorbing that I just sat back and enjoyed myself. But all the time, at the back of my mind, the kettle was boiling, the stairs a-climbing, and the roses getting dead-headed.

As I remember, it was a large-format magazine with text divided into three columns per page. I read the whole of the first page, then the second page and the third, and only when I found myself on the fourth page did my brain start to invent accusations against the journalist: You forgot! You forgot to tell us how long he can hold his breath!

But the writer hadn't forgotten, because at the top of the second column on that fourth page, he wrote something like: "You're probably wondering if I forgot to tell you how long he can hold his breath. I didn't. I was waiting. By now, if you read at the same speed as most people, you've been reading for X minutes. Well, that's how long wotsisname can hold his breath." As you see, I don't remember the actual number of minutes, or the diver's name, perhaps because although I was impressed by his prodigious lung capacity, I was even more impressed by the journalist's storytelling. It was so elegant! I loved it. It felt so good to be in the hands of somebody who referred to me, and my experience, as we were going along.

(Take note!) But to be clear: he didn't do that in a needy way. He wasn't desperate to please. On the contrary, he was teasing. He promised to reveal something remarkable in due course, and he did. Ever since then, much less skilfully than him, I always tried to do something similar: think of something remarkable in the story I'm telling, give a taste of it, and promise to come back to it later. After all, nobody has to read a magazine. It's optional. If a story doesn't hold them, they are free to go.

This has been a very long parenthesis. Before I move on to my gripping history of preaching in western Europe, I owe you a slender crescent of grammatical closure. I hope its absence hasn't been troubling you: I hadn't forgotten.

…)

## A short history of preaching in Western Europe

This section really is what the title says: a short history of preaching in Western Europe. You might not have guessed, when you picked up this book, that you needed a short history of preaching in Western Europe, and maybe when you've finished this section you'll decide that you didn't; but it can be refreshing and useful to draw lessons from a variety of disciplines. Whatever you happen to speak about, or plan to speak about, you may find something useful here. I hope so: as with the whole of this book, I urge you to take what you like and leave the rest.

If I sound a bit defensive, that's because preaching doesn't enjoy the prestige it commanded in other times and places, when thousands gathered in the open air to hear a famous preacher, and I'm conscious that you might be checking your watch, like the man beside me at David Kendall's after-dinner entertainment in Cambridge, which I'll come back to (see what I did there!). According to the *Tablet* magazine, this loss of prestige is because everyone these days wants to be heard, rather than listen, and attention spans are decreasing. Maybe so, maybe not. But times change, and preaching changes to meet different needs.

The homiletician (that is, teacher of preachers) Ron Boyd-Macmillan believes that sermons never do get much of a hearing when the living is easy. "The greatest change agent is always that ancient one, catastrophe," he says. It's to Boyd-MacMillan, and his excellent book *Explosive Preaching*, that I owe much of the following short history of preaching. "Preaching dark ages", he confidently adds, "have always been followed by preaching golden ages." (It just might not happen all at once. One of the dark ages, following the death of Pope Gregory the Great, lasted 600 years. Most priests couldn't read, and giving a sermon of your own was regarded as a little presumptuous.)

In the Old Testament, great preaching always starts with a celebration of God's greatness, moves on to a searing exposure of idolatry, gives life or death choices to listeners and finally makes clear what listeners must do/not do to please God. (Take away the references to God, and you have a blueprint for pretty well any speech: praise the good, condemn the bad, raise the stakes and present some choices. Ta da! The key difference between preachers and other speakers is that preachers retain the references to God.)

Moving on, he notes that Jesus preached with stories,

proverbs, finger-pointing ("woe to you...") and abstract propositions ("blessed are the poor"). Jesus shocked his audiences by the way he taught, the language he used, the things he did, the claims he made and the company he kept.

After Jesus came St Paul, whose letters employ the techniques of secular rhetoric, as outlined by Cicero. And then came the Church Fathers, including the well-named John Chrystostom (it means Golden Mouth), whose sermons involved going through Scripture one verse at a time. This scholarly approach, in unskilled hands, might lack drama but Origen and Augustine made their living teaching rhetoric and impressed people with their own, adds Boyd-MacMillan, not entirely suppressing a note of envy. "Where people today might ooh and aah over a spectacular feat by a footballer, back then they would whoop and yell appreciation for feats of language that would reach right into their heartstrings and elevate them to ecstasy."

Next, Aquinas made the sermon logical, using deduction – that is, starting out with a generally accepted proposition. Over time, this gradually gave way to the "moral essay" sermon, which stressed the ethical benefits of Christianity, providing the listener with something to do. When this became stale, evangelical revivalism sought to make the gospel dramatic, and move the emotions of the listener. A leading exponent, George Whitefield, memorised his sermons and improvised, pacing about, weeping, acting out passages from the gospels with different voices and gestures, and drew tens of thousands to his outdoor sermons, many of them people who had given up on traditional churches. This kind of sermon is highly individual: you couldn't give your text to somebody else and expect them to deliver it for you. For that reason, it's also the biggest test of a preacher's ego.

Then came the liberal inductive sermon which, like scientific enquiry, begins with the observation of particulars, and moves to a general hypothesis.

In 1971, against a background of widespread resistance to power, and a rejection of time-honoured traditions, Fred Craddock published a book on homiletics that had a big impact: in *As One Without Authority*, he urged preachers to enlist their listeners in co-discovering truth, rather than risk talking down to them.

Why do I find all this fascinating? Because nowhere else can I find an account of how relatively ordinary people have spoken and presented to other relatively ordinary people, and how that has changed over time. I'm fascinated that my ancestors could have been so gripped, and to be reminded that we too may be gripped one day, perhaps not far off, by approaches and styles ill-suited to the here and now; and to think that people might once again ooh and aah at the sound of a spoken phrase.

And I'm especially delighted that this historical survey of preaching terminates in what might easily be described as the early 21st century's secular equivalent of revivalist extravaganzas: the TED talk, and its less prestigious sibling, the TEDx.

## Secular inductive sermons

When I told friends I was writing a book about speaking and presenting, one said she hoped it would help to put an end to the kind of talks in which the speaker says, "I've been on quite a journey..."

TED and TEDx talks, which from now I'll just call TED talks, have been extraordinarily successful, winning billions of views online and quite a large number in real life. Most are inductive secular sermons, structured as stories, in which the speaker describes learning something over a period of time. "I did this, it went wrong, I tried this, it still didn't work, and when I was about to give up, I tried this other thing, and it was a triumph, and I'm here today to share my 'journey' with you and save you from making the same mistakes I did."

Many speakers deliberately structure their story using what is called the Hero's Journey, much loved by screenwriters in Hollywood. The Hero's Journey is a framework originally codified by an anthropologist called Joseph Campbell in a book that I confess I found unreadable, and therefore haven't read. People who (claim to) have read it say that Campbell made a study of stories from all over the world, and throughout history, leading him to notice certain patterns. For instance, the hero is often a nobody, and feels unqualified for the task ahead. In many instances, the hero is given his (sometimes her) task, plus a specific object, by a wise older person (Gandalf gives a ring to Frodo in *The Lord of the Rings*, Obi-Wan Kenobi gives a light-sabre to Luke Skywalker in *Star Wars*). For a long period after that, the hero has a dreadfully tough time of it and wants to give up – then has an even tougher time – but finally prevails.

Hurrah!

So far as this goes, it's helpful and useful to people who have no idea how to structure a story. But while we like to see similarities, we also enjoy finding difference. A story that is too obviously structured along these lines is boring and predictable. If it is formulaic, it will probably also seem synthetic, fake, heartless. So learning the "secret" of the Hollywood scriptwriters (as Campbell's idea is frequently described) is no good if you don't also learn how to build around it, hide it, creating something that is fresh, honest and uniquely yours.

## Fresh and honest

But how do you know what to put in? In case you've forgotten – which would be my fault, so please forgive me – this chapter is about the content of your speech: Choose Really Interesting Proofy Evidence Stuff.

What, of all the things you know, might be interesting to others? Ultimately, you can never know. But you can focus on what's interesting to you. And that means learning to trust your intuition – something hard for adults but easy for young children. Children know instinctively what makes a good story.

A few years ago, I went into a primary school to talk to eight-year-olds about journalism. To begin, I told them a bit about what I had done myself (briefly, lest their eyes should glaze over), then moved on to describe how it works, with editors sending the likes of me out to interview people and write up a story.

Then we did a practical exercise. I asked one of the children to be my deputy editor, and to bring me two cracking stories for the following day's paper – by asking her classmates to interview each other. This proved to be an excellent demonstration of getting to the heart of a story, finding the "ooh!" moment, instead of being all obscure and sophisticated like grown-ups.

First, she asked a boy to interview a girl about her time in the Brownies. The idea was to show how a "generalist" reporter (that is, not a specialist in the subject) tries to get something interesting out of the encounter. It went very well.

"What was the most scariest thing that you ever did when you were a Brownie?" was his first question.

"Well, once we were jumping over a bin and I fell straight into the bin and it tipped over head first," she replied. There was much wild laughter before the reporter could continue and flush out details such as whether or not the Brownie came out smelly (she didn't).

At the end, we role-played what happens after interviews are finished. My deputy editor "phoned" her reporter to find out how the interview had gone, asking for highlights. Then I, in the persona of hard-to-impress big-chief editor (not based on any real person, living or dead), phoned the junior editor to find out from her what the story was.

Interestingly, some circumstantial details of the original story were mangled in this telephone relay. "That may partly explain why people complain that newspapers get things wrong," I said. "Simple misunderstanding."

I asked the class what the headline should be. A boy at the back suggested a headline that seemed spot on: "A Brownie fell in a dustbin." (There was some debate about whether readers might think this was a story about a chocolate brownie, but the consensus was that a photo of the Brownie in question would remove any ambiguity.)

For the next exercise, I asked my youthful deputy to organise an interview by a specialist reporter. Two boys volunteered to discuss their shared enthusiasm for cars. The conversation, recorded on my phone, went exactly as follows:

"What was the fastest speed you ever experienced in a car?"

"A hundred and thirty-two miles an hour in my dad's car."

"Where was it, on a motorway?"

"The M4."

"Was there a traffic jam?"

"No, but there was a Jaguar in front of us doing about 30 miles an hour – a hundred less than us."

"Was it day time or night time?"

"Day time."

"Where were you going to?"

"Cornwall."

"Was there anybody else in the car?"

"Just me and my dad."

I was amazed by the interviewer's skill, and the interviewee's unguarded willingness to provide such a scoop. I was dismayed that the stories we had come up with, like any downmarket tabloid, had focused on disaster and lawbreaking. Perhaps this just confirms what the tabloids argue: that This Is What They Want.

## You aren't eight years old

Unless I am gravely mistaken, most people reading this book

are not eight years old. Most (assuming that there are any other readers apart from you, special one) will have gone into, and emerged from, teenage awkwardness with an abiding sense that they can't just go around telling people they fell in a dustbin, or drove to Cornwall at nearly twice the legal speed limit. Most people are less comfortable about sharing stories of such a revealing nature.

But if stories don't make you feel at least a teeny bit awkward, they're probably Very Boring Indeed.

In a TED talk that was viewed by millions, the American academic Brené Brown, an authority on vulnerability and shame, asked the live audience in front of her two questions. First: "How many of you struggle to be vulnerable because you think of vulnerability as weakness?" Hands shot up around the room. Second: "When you watch people on this stage being vulnerable, how many of you thought it was courageous?" Again, hands shot up around the room.

I had the pleasure of interviewing Brown for the *Guardian* not long afterwards. I sat at my desk, in London, getting only mildly dizzy as I watched her through the camera on a computer that she walked around her home in (I think) Texas. She summarised the point she made in the TED talk: "We like to experience other people's vulnerability, but we don't want to be vulnerable ourselves."

To overcome that, she said, we need to develop resilience to shame: "Because we can't allow ourselves to be seen if we're terrified about what people might think. Shame derives its power from being unspeakable. That's why it loves perfectionists. When you develop shame resilience, you still want folks to like, respect and even admire what you have created, but your self-worth is not on the table."

To paraphrase: you can tell people you fell in a dustbin, without thinking it makes you a bad person.

## Play with the structure

Generally speaking, stories are more interesting if they don't just start at the beginning and deliver every fact and incident in strict chronological order.

Once, I watched five improvisers line up on stage. They all represented the same individual, but at five different points in her life.

The person in the middle represented a central moment of great importance: her wedding. The ones on either side spoke for that same woman exactly one day before the wedding and one day after. The outer figures represented the distant past – childhood at one end and old age at the other.

This being improvisation, there was no script. Participants created the story by using whatever had been said already, and either confirming or overturning audience expectations. The woman in the middle started them off.

"Today at last all I hoped for comes true!" she said.

The person representing her one day later spoke next: "Where has he gone? And where is my jewellery?" (Don't expect me to tell you where this idea came from. Nobody knows where ideas come from. God put it there. Or, if you will, "God".)

Next to speak was the person representing the distant past, the woman-when-she-was-a-child. "Mummy died today. Before she died she gave me her wedding ring and told me I must promise to wear it when I get married, and always remember her."

Cut to the person at the other end, representing the old lady: "When they found him, he had been dead for weeks."

Can you see how breaking up the ordinary sequence of events can be startling and exciting?

It's not necessary to break it up, because even a flat-footed summary would contain poignancy, even tragedy: "Recently, police found the body of my husband, with the wedding ring given to me by my mother before she died, which he stole one day after our wedding."

Even telling the story chronologically it would be more than OK: "When I was a girl, my mother gave me her wedding ring just before she died. I was so happy on my wedding day to wear the ring. But when I woke the following day it had disappeared, along with my husband. When he was found with the ring, decades later, he was dead."

What distinguishes the improvised version is the element of surprise – the way it hoiks the audience through an unexpected sequence of emotional experience. What does this mean for you, and your stories? Everything! Because how you choose to arrange your story can make a tremendous difference to what your audience thinks and feels. If you want people to start sad and move towards happiness, you tell it one way. To start buoyant and finish deflated, arrange the same story differently.

Happy to sad: "I was never so happy as on my wedding day, when my husband eased onto my finger the ring that had been given to me by my mother. I had no idea that one day later all would be lost – the ring, and my husband with it. For the next 30 years I lived entirely alone."

Sad to happy: "The wedding ring my mother gave me before she died was stolen by the man I married. Recently, having been separated from it for three decades, I was reunited with it."

(You won't have failed to notice that, in order to achieve these effects, certain details have been omitted, and others emphasised.)

Chris Toumazis and his brother, at their sister's wedding, combined heartfelt sentiment with humour. Typically, wedding speeches move from comic material to sentiment, and I'm sure you can guess why. Reverse that at your peril.

Dadaists used to make poetry by placing words randomly in sequence, leaving their readers to find patterns and make whatever sense of it they could. You may wish to do the same yourself with your storytelling – or indeed your speaking and presenting in general. But I recommend that you consider, if only to reject the idea later, what effect you would like to have and build a talk that's most likely to achieve that.

David Kendall, the after-dinner speaker, having successfully delivered his comic material after many dinners over a very long time, probably didn't need to alter it for that gala in Cambridge. But there's one thing worth mentioning about his approach that evening: he would follow the advice given him by a friend, formerly warm-up man for a TV presenter, about speaking down south: "First, retain the Yorkshire accent. Second, stick to northern gags. Don't be witty and sophisticated. They don't want you to be Stephen Fry."

It's worth pausing over this. Novice speakers might assume they should try to "fit in" with their audience. Maybe, maybe not. What really matters is the audience's expectations, which you can choose to meet or overturn, depending on what you want to achieve.

At Downing College, after the chairman rose to propose a toast ("The Queen!"), and a short prize-giving ceremony, Kendall was introduced as the evening's entertainment.

He rose from his seat, without ceasing to probe inside his ear with his index finger, and for a period of not less than 40 minutes he mined his hoard of gags and stories. A man on my table, sitting with the thoughtful air of a connoisseur, shook his head regretfully every so often and did his best to undermine Kendall by audibly muttering punchlines before they fell due. But even this man laughed at jokes he'd not heard before.

Others laughed with relish; even uncontrollably. Kendall's gags may not have been particularly challenging, but despite that – or because of it – the punters seemed unlikely to ask for their money back.

After about 30 minutes, a woman on the top table was

lost to hysterics, but I noticed the man beside me check his watch. Having presumably concluded that Kendall had not tired him out – yet – he put his glasses back on and carried on laughing.

## Something confessional

I've chosen another speech for you to examine, and take apart. It's by another Brit, but a woman this time, and not somebody with the high official status of a Churchill. It's more confessional, and includes personal stories. You might want to pay particular attention to how the speaker handles those.

As ever, you need to read it first – and at least once aloud.

Look for the speaker's subject, argument and purpose.

Consider what she does to establish her Credentials. What comes under the heading of Reasoning? (Logic, facts, opinions, timelines, laws, rules, all that.)

And Emotion? What emotional responses do you have, and when? How does the speaker use stories to achieve that?

Does she use cliffhangers? Are the stories delivered straight, from start to finish? Does she "fall in a dustbin" or "break the speed limit" (that is, are there any "ooh!" moments)? Does she show herself to be vulnerable, in the way Brené Brown described? This in particular is something you will sense more clearly if you read the speech aloud. Don't ask me why, but if it moves you, you're more likely to get a catch in your throat. (I never heard somebody say they got a catch in their brain.)

The talk is one of those "secular inductive sermons" I mentioned: a TEDx. It was delivered in 2015 in London, to an event organised by and particularly for women. The speaker is my friend Tazeen Ahmad, and I'm not going to give any comments. You're on your own with this one.

## "On Going Blank", Tazeen Ahmad
*TEDx Hackney Women, 2 July 2015*

It was the spring of 2012. It was a wet, cold, windy night. I was out covering yet another story on the upcoming Olympics.

The cab driver got lost. I was navigating, I was writing my story, I was speaking to my editor in New York. The cab driver was lost, I was moved from one location to another, writing my story, rewriting my story, dealing with my editor in New York. At close to midnight, I finally stopped. I stood in the cold, and the wet, and the wind, near Tower Bridge, camera and lights upon me. But this time, unusually for me, I was a bit more stressed and discombobulated than normal.

I'm a television journalist. I've worked undercover, I've worked and lived in dangerous parts of the world, I do live shows all the time. I've also worked on big programmes that get very carefully scrutinised. I give talks on stages, at conferences, at lecture halls. I've been doing this for two decades and working under pressure is pretty much second nature for me.

So, there I was. I stood in position, camera and lights on me. Five, four, three, two, one. I heard in my ear, "Cue Tazeen" – and I went blank.

I couldn't think. All my words, the carefully rehearsed

script I had put together, just disappeared.

I tried desperately to recall them as the audience of America's most-watched news programme watched me. Still nothing. Then I ad-libbed, and I ad-libbed very poorly. After ten of the longest seconds of my life, finally the producers cut to the piece I was trying to introduce. I can't imagine for a second the conversation that took place in the control room. I try not to think about it too much, but I imagine it wasn't very flattering and it probably involved a lot of expletives. Then I came off air, and my producer called me and he said, "What the heck happened?"

"I don't know," I said, genuinely bewildered. "I just don't know."

I'm a journalist who's been trained to work in hostile environments, and the training says that if you're thrown into the deep, dark unknown, take three deep breaths. If a bomb goes off and you need to scarper, or leave, or think about what to do next: take three deep breaths. If someone is terribly injured and you need to help: take three deep breaths. The sudden onset of stress starves your brain of oxygen. If you need to think properly and function properly, you need to give it oxygen.

Until that moment in the spring of 2012, I had never forgotten my words on air. Five years ago, in 2010, I experienced a trauma the scale of which was so horrifying and so enormous that for a long time I couldn't even describe it. In order to protect my privacy and the privacy of those who were also involved and affected, I cannot share it and I will never share it, but what I will share is what it did to me. In a key moment, stress flooded my body, adrenaline kicked in, and when I look back, that's what I remember. Thinking absolutely nothing, and feeling a tsunami of adrenaline flooding me.

I took a breath and shock stole that breath away from me for ever. At the same time, it slammed a metaphorical sledgehammer right where my memory lay.

I don't recall what happened next. I know it, but I can't recall it. "Dissociative amnesia", "psychogenic amnesia", "traumatic amnesia". There are so many names for it, it's as powerful as being concussed, say psychologists. For me, in simple terms, it just means that I forget.

I grew up with trauma. To cope, as a child, I disassociated. The result of which was the areas where my memory was stored and processed in my brain became damaged. But soon childhood was over and I recovered and my brain recovered. Then five years ago I was thrust into terror and darkness again.

What happened was bad enough, but what it left me with was utterly, utterly, debilitating. It's a wound that nobody can see. So now, I forget things. My memory goes blank every day. I grapple in the dark, in the darkness of my mind to try and remember, and I struggle to store new information. I knew that I'd fail to recall the words for this talk, so I broke the rules, and like in all my public speaking, I have my precious notes with me.

I can rely on my research, I can rely on my writing. I can't rely on being able to retain or to keep memory, remember memory.

Once I forgot my own name. I was with a friend, and we were in a rural area and he disappeared 100 or 200 yards down the road to a wedding hall. He had to pop in and drop something off. While I was waiting in the dark, in the cold, wet, windy dark – there's something in that right? Keeps happening to me! – while I was waiting in the dark, I started to... I think I got a little scared. It was dark and it was late. I started thinking, what if someone comes over and says, "What are you doing here? What's your name? Who are you?" And I said, "What's my name? What's my name? What's my name?"

Round and round I spun, thinking: "What's my name? What's my name? Mary? Susan? Louise?" No. After 20, 30 minutes he came back, he sat in the driver's seat and he turned to me casually and said, "Hi Tazeen. Sorry about that. You OK?"

Ah, I thought. "That's my name."

Another time, I was walking around in Victoria in central London, an area that I know well. I go there all the time, I worked there a lot, and I came out of a building that I know well. I looked around me and I couldn't figure out where I was. I didn't know where I was going and I didn't know what I was doing there. I looked at the buildings and they were familiar to me as buildings, but I didn't know where I was going. I didn't know where I was supposed to be. I thought, Tube station! Get to a Tube station! And I started walking round and round in circles, literally in circles, on the same street.

I was just around the corner from Victoria Tube Station. I know it really well. But that day I had no idea. Other times, I've forgotten really obvious information about myself. What I was doing, what I need to do next.

Thoughts that I scramble to retain leave me far too soon. I am buried in a mountain of Post-its at home. By the way, this isn't everyday forgetfulness. The NHS website says, "Someone with dissociative amnesia will repeatedly have periods they cannot remember key information about themselves or about events. These gaps in memory are much more severe than normal forgetfulness. These blank episodes may last minutes, they may last hours, or they may last days." I affectionately call these memory blanks my "black holes".

"Hang on a second, I just need to write that down before I forget it," is my most overused phrase. My kids will put it on my tombstone, I'm quite sure of it. I have lots of tricks. I walk around with a pen, I write memos in my hand, I have some today. I rely on notes. I do my pieces to camera in two or three shots. I ad-lib them if I have to, if I can, so I don't need to recall a script, and I rely on me, my passion, my writing, my research, my knowledge. So yeah, childhood trauma and adult trauma, combined, does that to the mind.

The hippocampus, where memory is formed and processed and stored, gets damaged and it shrinks, so my body has kept score of what I've been through. Here are the top four things I've learned about trauma. Number one, it feels like a bomb blast to the life, to body and mind. It overwhelms you in its flames and there is no respite.

Number two, 80 per cent of people will suffer a traumatic event in their life. Ergo, we are more likely to experience a traumatic event than not. One in four kids will experience an event that will go on to affect them throughout their lives. Twenty-five to thirty per cent will experience a traumatic event, which will then, or may, develop into a serious disorder.

Number three, trauma can strike at any time. Nobody is immune. A terrible accident, a violent attack, a natural disaster, a war, anything extreme, inexplicable, unexpected and horrific, are its key traits.

Number four, one of the most violating aspects in the aftermath of trauma is hearing, not just from the authorities but also from people you love, and who love you dearly, "It's over now. You've got to move on with your life." I'm not a scientist, I'm not going to show you before and after pictures of the brain. I'm not going to explain what happens to the brain of a traumatised person, although that's not to say I don't understand it very well.

I have a pile of books this high on trauma. I'm a student of psychology and psychotherapy now. I have read an endless number of journals on neuroscience and the brain's plasticity. I've almost completed a certificate in psychotraumatology and I'm a member of the UK Psychological Trauma Society, as well as the European Society for Traumatic Stress Studies. If I was going to be afflicted with this, I was going to understand it the best way I could.

So, here's how I responded to my life's events. I find myself looking for kindred spirits and I found them in our greatest writers. "In a real dark night of the soul, it is always three o'clock in the morning, day after day," said F Scott Fitzgerald, and I chose this because it sums up the private hell of trauma. I've been drawn to dark stories all my life. Subconsciously, I didn't realize it. I was working on one story after the other that was dark and terrible. Then I started to do it consciously after this event five years ago. I started to look for those [dark side] stories because I wanted to tell those stories. I turned into the Darth Vader of storytelling.

I've interviewed hundreds of people over the years who experienced something so terrible that they too temporarily lost their minds. I'd like to honour their experiences by just telling you about a few of them right now. The parents whose daughter was killed in a vicious honour killing. The man who quietly told me about how he went into hospital with his pregnant wife who had stomach cramps and she bled to death in front of him. The young woman viciously raped over four years by gangs of men. Seventy-two men in total. The amazing cop who put his life in danger for 20 years infiltrating pitiful groups. The father whose beloved son went to Afghanistan to fight jihad unbeknownst to him, and then disappeared for ever. The mothers whose children were abused by the very man they had fallen in love with and married. The couple kidnapped by pirates, never knowing if they'd be freed. And the teenager abducted by the Taliban in ultra-conservative Pakistan, raped by local police and by the men who abducted her, left pregnant, and when she fought bravely for justice, her brother was shot dead in front of her.

Trauma has so many ugly faces and all of these extraordinary people have faced one of the most hideous sides of life. After trauma, as if to add insult to injury, there's more hideousness. Here's what the traumatised are left with. Uncontrollable physical conditions, anger, numbness, hypervigilance, fear, fatigue, flashbacks, lack of concentration, lack of confidence, lack of trust, despair, fogginess, depression, anxiety, panic attacks, shame, guilt, stress, nightmares and memory failure. For me professionally, the most brutal blow was memory loss. Personally, I swung between numbness and hypervigilance and terrifying nightmares. But look, today is not just for me about telling you about the bad news and the ugliness. I also want to tell you about something really fantastic and amazing.

"The world breaks everyone and afterwards, some are strong at the broken places," said Ernest Hemingway.

Over the last 20 years, psychologists and the scientific community are talking about something called post-traumatic growth. In other words, the gift of adversity. Those people I met, those people I interviewed, they didn't want what had happened to them to have happened in vain, so some campaigned for changes in the law. Others spoke out to shed light, to expose. They took new jobs, they took new roles, and they gave their life new meaning.

After 9/11, researchers found that 58 per cent of people found that there were personal and existential benefits. Life felt more precious, people were kinder to each other.

After life kicked me in the teeth, I found renewed purpose. I started to lobby on things I really care about. I use my profile to do that. I help others with their campaigns. I work to improve my life and that of others. I've done more public speaking on things I care about in the last year than I have done in two decades of television.

Post-traumatic growth is very controversial. There's not a consensus about it, and there's a lot of talk about not being able to measure it. Some say that talking about the opportunity the trauma gives and provides is an insult to those who have suffered. I say, "If you've got a silver lining, please hand it over."

Of course, you would not have wanted to have suffered in the first place. Of course, you may remain haunted for years. But in the midst of it, you can develop new perspectives and new capabilities. And I think that's amazing.

This is how psychologists describe post-traumatic growth. There's a trauma, and the life around it, it takes up a lot of space, as you can see. As post-traumatic growth happens, the trauma doesn't get smaller, it stays the same size, but life grows around it. Your life gets bigger as you heal. I think this is really exciting and I think this is really hopeful. It is not true for everyone, but it is definitely true for me. You'll note that I have not said PTSD. I think the term has become so medicalised, so depersonalised, so stigmatised, so closely associated only with war veterans and soldiers, that today I want you to think of it as adversity, as traumatic experiences, as losing one's mind. How did I mend? Well, first of all, I did a lot of grieving, I processed my memories, I read a lot, I did a lot of writing therapy, I did a lot of therapy therapy with two amazing women at the Tavistock who literally saved my life. Meditation, exercise, sleep, human connection, intimacy, friendship, laughter, love, friendship, laughter, love and lots and lots and lots of memory tricks.

Then I made changes in my professional life. I took on only stories I really cared about or that were fun or enlightening to work on. I turned my other interests into work, emotional intelligence, emotional health, psychology, psychotherapy, helping others find how to live a deeper, more fulfilling life. So yeah, I got myself a little bit of that PTD. When you have therapy for trauma, they get you to picture a place that makes you feel safe, where you can go in your mind, a place that gets you away from the terrible memories that can flood you. This is my beautiful, comforting bookshelf where I read and read and read and read and read.

I did a lot of reading and a lot of walking. What would I suggest for others? Learn a new skill, do things you love. This builds new pathways in the brain. Tell your story again and again, until it loses its grip on you, to a journal, to professionals, to people you trust. Leave no stone unturned. Know that you'll get control of your body and your mind again. Laugh hard, love deep, and bring your friends close. You can never go back, so you need to embrace forward momentum. Evidence shows people who have been through hell care a lot less about what others will think of them. Be that person.

Emily Dickinson said, "After great pain, a formal feeling comes. The nerves sit ceremonious like tombs," and I sort of feel like this is where I am now. I'm feeling, starting to feel formidable on the inside.

I'm a little bit ashamed and quite proud of the story I'm going to tell you. I was on the London Tube, on the ground at Kings Cross on the escalators, and there were three people in front of me, and they started to stumble. As they started to stumble, their luggage, they were slightly older, so they were struggling to keep a grip. They started to stumble, they were having a domino effect, so they were going to fall on me, I was next.

What did I do? I didn't reach out to try and help. I didn't try and help them with their luggage. Other people were doing that. I coolly stepped aside, literally pushing the woman next to me out of the way as I did that.

I thought to myself, "Oh my goodness, my survival instinct is so strong that I will step out of the way of disaster and not potentially plummet to my death."

And then I thought, "Oh my goodness, my survival instinct is so strong that I will step out of the way and I will let other people potentially plummet to their death!" It's kind of disgusting, and I do think it's disgusting, but I'm also proud of it – because I wouldn't have done this before. I'd have been frozen. That was my survival instinct. Now, I'm more resilient, from what I've been through. And clearly, if disaster were to strike again, I can take care of myself.

What are the things I'd like you to take away from today? We all need to talk about trauma because we could all be affected by it. Remember, 80 per cent of people!, we need it to stop being a shameful, invisible wound. It is too big and it is too bloody to hide it. We need to respect it like we do all physical illnesses. I would never have hoped for adversity or trauma to have visited my life, not in childhood and not now. It was terrible and it was earth shattering, and I wish it had never happened. But, I also hope that I am living, breathing, positive proof, that Ralph Waldo Emerson was right when he said, "When it is dark enough, you can see the stars."

Thank you.

## Torture the hero

Keith said to his audience of would-be improvisers: "What's the definition of a victim?"

Hands went up. Answers were given. Keith sat on his prop sofa, which has a secret slit in its back so that performers can disappear in the middle of a scene. He chewed over what we said. Waited a bit. Built up the tension.

"A victim is a man in a hole," he said eventually, then continued to ruminate. The longer the silence, the wiser he seemed. (Take note.)

"And what is the definition of a hero?"

The same routine ensued: hands up, answers out, chewing over. Again none of the answers, which touched on risk-taking, being young and good-looking and fighting dragons, were what he wanted.

"A hero is a man in a hole, trying to get out."

Long pause. Massive sense of drama. Whatever does he mean?

"If you let the hero out of the hole, the story's over. You

must keep torturing the hero. Keep pushing him back in the hole. Or let him out but only to fall immediately into another one."

The significance of this is hard to overstate. If your hero gets out of the hole, tension evaporates. Your audience relaxes, wonders when the coffee break is coming.

Empathy invites audiences to expect: to wish or to dread. Depending on how you fulfil or deny those expectations, audiences respond with disappointment, relief, horror or delight. This is instinctive, because stories are in our bones. We learn about the world, as children, through stories, and we know when they end as instinctively as we recognise the end of a sentence.

This doesn't apply only to children's stories, fables and legends, like *Star Wars* (where the "hole" is Luke's mission to save Princess Leia) or *The Lord of the Rings* (where the hole is Frodo's journey to deliver the ring to Mount Doom). It applies equally to dainty tales of everyday middle-class life, and the most intricate accounts of intellectual obscurity. Authors who torture their heroes include Jane Austen, George Eliot and Henry James.

A story can, of course, have several heroes. Soap operas keep going for ever because they always keep at least two or three people in a hole, trying to get out (have an affair without being caught, avoid bankruptcy, escape an abuser). It's useful to know this if you are doing a series of talks or presentations: keeping one of your stories unresolved, with a hero trying to get out of a hole, will sustain interest between the first talk and the next.

But if you are doing only one 60-minute talk, don't leave

anybody in a hole at the end. Get them all out, and let them take a bow.

The speech by Winston Churchill didn't use a great deal of story. But there were glimpses. Remember the doughty servicemen he mentioned, doing their exercises without equipment? Can you see how he used them to twiddle the empathy switch on his fellow MPs? In Tazeen's speech, the sense of a person in a hole (to state the bleedin' obvious, it doesn't have to be a man), must have been clear.

Who will be your hero – or heroes? It could be you (it probably will be, at least a little), but it could also be a friend, ally, dependant, or colleague. It could even be a rival. If you produce a certain kind of product, and you are pitching to a potential client, you might look incredibly confident, generous and likeable if you tell a story about an individual in a rival company who struggled for a long time with a problem related to that product, and eventually overcame it. But make sure to add that your company, too, these days, has learned to do the same (and at a cheaper price, with bells on).

## What happened in Mexico

At that conference in Mexico, walking with the famous people towards lunch, something caught my eye. It was a kind of human-sized hamster wheel, with a blown-up image of planet earth inside it.

Without thinking through what I was about to do, I turned to the man walking beside me, the husband of the woman whose real life had been turned into several series of TV drama, and handed him my phone. "Hey, can you film me?"

I guess that the picture of the earth made me think about my book title, *How to Change the World*. And I had a hazy notion that a film of me walking in this hamster wheel, making the globe turn, might make a cheery little video to send to my daughter. But I spent less time thinking about it than it has taken me to write this sentence. The famous people were walking fast towards lunch, and I didn't want to get left behind, nor to delay my friend the husband-of-the-woman-who.

So I got into the hamster wheel and started walking, at a cheerfully brisk pace.

And in less than a second I knew this was a terrible mistake. The wheel turned without impediment, getting faster with every step. It was going to be impossible to stay upright. The only uncertainty was how long it might take for me to – bang, crash, wallop.

I fell on my face and banged my head very painfully. Two of the most famous people were right beside me, and I heard one of them say, "Oh my goodness!" and lean over me. I lay prone, for a few moments, dizzy and wondering if I might have broken anything. Security guards rushed over and held the wheel to stop it turning further. Some of the famous people helped me to my feet. I stood, dazed, insisting that I was alright and holding my face in a smiling mask that didn't conceal my embarrassment, as I know because the whole thing, right up to this moment, was being filmed by the husband-of-the-woman-who.

He pressed the "stop" button and walked over, asked if I was OK and handed me the phone.

I felt so ashamed. But I kept smiling.

At lunchtime, I sat next to the famous woman who had said "Oh my goodness". By now, we were having a tasty lunch. The conversation around the table was upbeat. When dessert arrived – a green jelly that quivered like I did – she said something about my tumble that briefly cheered me up a teeny bit.

"It's unusual to see somebody make themselves so vulnerable – like Brené Brown, but with more physical comedy."

But after lunch I went back to the hotel and sank into shame again (Brené Brown could have predicted that).

I sat on my bed, took my phone out, put it away again, then out and back away several times.

Eventually I watched the short video. I simply couldn't bring myself to watch the last bit. I thought I might vomit, and remember actually shoving the phone away from me.

What kind of an idiot was I? What was I doing here?

After mouldering in sickliness for some minutes, I phoned Steve Chapman in London and told him what had happened. He said, "Oh!" Then, "I'm sure it feels awful, but what a wonderful thing to have on film. Why don't you show the audience tomorrow?"

It was a terrible, brilliant idea.

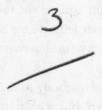

# STYLE

## Clear out rubbish but leave
## it massively elegant

*It was astonishing how figures of speech crowded upon him.
He was like a man in an orchard, where boughs loaded
with fruit hung around him, and he pulled apples as fast
as he pleased and pelted the ministry.*

James Boswell

## Read my lips

You will recall that Rachel Ison, the stunningly successful first-timer, took care to read her speech beforehand to her mother, then to her father and anybody else who was around. Rebecca Twomey, before speaking as her friend's "father of the bride", did the same.

This is a time-honoured tradition. Two thousand years ago, poets gathered to read each other work in progress, sometimes for hours, sometimes whole days on end. This was about as welcome for some as it might be for you: Pliny the

Younger is on record getting very cross indeed about guests who retreated to an annex, leaving only a servant to listen and tip them off when proceedings were drawing to a close. In the opinion of Pliny the Younger, the feedback process was mutual. That was the deal.

Alas, today, it's hard to find others who are planning talks and presentations at the same time as you, willing to sit through yours and exchange feedback. We're all busy.

But then, it has also been a tradition to read aloud from work in progress, in hope of useful feedback, without the process being mutual. Twelve hundred years after Pliny, Geoffrey Chaucer read *The Canterbury Tales* aloud, making note of heckles and incorporating them into the work itself, as dialogue between his pilgrim storytellers.

Charles Dickens read his final drafts to groups of friends for similar reasons; and rejoiced (in letters to his wife) if he made people cry.

Reading aloud to others can feel awkward, but it's more valuable than reading to yourself. "I feel weak places at once," wrote Samuel Butler, "where I thought when I read to myself only that the passage was alright."

If all else fails, at least read your words aloud to yourself. You might also record them, and listen back as an imaginary audience. "Nobody who has not habitually done so," wrote the late Kingsley Amis, "can imagine the farrago of ineptitudes revealed by this obvious method – unintended rhymes, assonances and repetitions, continual failure of whatever organ might guard against bad sound. If a paragraph of prose is to sound satisfying to its reader's inner or outer ear, it must already have satisfied its writer by the same criteria."

On a residential writing course where I sometimes teach, the highlight is always the final evening, when participants read a polished fragment of work in progress to each other, and get feedback.

This goes particularly well because we have agreed on the terms of the feedback.

If you just read something to somebody and say, "What do you think?" they won't be able to help much, and are liable to come out with something kind but unhelpful, or unkind and unhelpful. Remember that feedback can be awkward for both recipient and giver, so make it easier for everybody by saying exactly what kind of advice you're after. "Vulnerability is at the heart of the feedback process," says Brené Brown, "whether we give, receive or solicit feedback. It doesn't go away if we're trained, but experience gives us the advantage of knowing we can survive the exposure and uncertainty."

When I ask for feedback, I ask people two things:

What did you like?

What would you like more?

## A daily miracle

If you think about it, it's amazing that people don't run away whenever another person opens their mouth to speak.

Because from a scientific perspective, Stephen Pinker says, we have no right to expect to understand what is about to hit us in the ears. (I paraphrase.) If a person is capable of producing sentences up to 20 words long, Pinker calculates, then they might at any time produce any of one hundred million trillion sentences.

From the listener's point of view, that ought to be terrifying. Why isn't it?

One reason is that the number falls dramatically as soon as the first word is uttered, and again with every word that follows. And then each sentence. Each new sentence opens up a vast new horizon, but if the speaker is a relatively normal human being, it is likely to follow more or less logically from the sentence that preceded it.

If you interrupt a speaker at random, Pinker calculates, there could be just one word that could possibly follow, or thousands. But the average is about ten.

I have no idea how he did the maths, but I've spent a lot of time examining that moment of verbal uncertainty, in another simple game taught by Keith Johnstone. In this exercise, participants make up a story, one word at a time. The first four words are easy and predictable:

"Once..."

"...upon..."

"...a..."

"...time..."

But the person who comes fifth has to make a choice. Usually the safe choice:

"...there..."

And you know what the next word is likely to be:

"...was..."

It could have been any verb in the past tense. "Once upon a time there flew/burned/screamed..." But safety leads participants, especially nervous participants, to choose "was".

Mind you, safety is boring. So eventually somebody comes out with something risky.

"Once upon a time there was a young man who wanted to..."

"...tickle..." (or "prance", "snort", or any number of other things).

Whenever somebody utters a word that is even slightly risky, the whole group laughs, delighted. But if it happens too often, they lose interest. Stories are made by variously fulfilling and upending the audience's expectations. Fulfil too often and it's boring. Upend all the time and it's chaos, which becomes boring. In a previous chapter we saw that this applies to your talk at the structural level: which story do you tell first?

Playing the word-at-a-time game shows that it also applies to the sentence or phrase.

The reason we don't freak out at the thought of our interlocutor's hundred million trillion sentences is simple: we understand sentences one word at a time. That's how simultaneous translation is possible.

It was pioneered at the Nuremberg trials, and halved the time the trials would otherwise have taken.

To see how astonishing this is, ask somebody to speak to you, and follow their lips so that you repeat what they say almost exactly as they speak. It's not easy, but it's possible. Then imagine that additionally you must render their words into another language. Compared with this, merely listening to a platform speaker from the comfort of the audience seems relatively simple. But even that is impossible with sentences that are badly built.

A badly built sentence requires the listener to hold in mind more than is humanly possible. Pinker calls these "garden path" sentences, because they lead the listener up the garden path. Bearing in mind the pain they inflict, he could have chosen a name more redolent of crime. Here's an example Pinker gives in his excellent book *The Language Instinct*:

"He gave the girl that he met in New York while visiting his parents for ten days around Christmas and New Year the candy."

Can you imagine translating that in real time? To make sense of it, I suspect that you had to read it more than once. Plainly, that's impossible if the sentence is spoken aloud. With live speakers, you can't press rewind.

As Amis pointed out, far too many writers don't say their sentences aloud. The other day, looking for garden path sentences, I opened a copy of the day's newspaper at random and copied out the first sentence of every news story. A surprising number were garden path sentences.

The first sentence in the first story on the front page read like this: "More than 11,000 women treated by a rogue surgeon jailed for maiming patients will be called in for checks as a report prompted calls for an urgent review of private health care."

I don't know about you, but I think that sentence is confusing, and too long. If you used it in a talk or presentation, would listeners be impressed?

Of course, some first sentences were readable and intriguing, making me want to read more. "On a royal day out, anything can happen." (Ooh, what can the writer mean? What a tease!)

Or, "The mayor of Compton, California, looked out at her hometown crowd and stated: 'New times call for new tactics.'" (Gosh, what's the mayor going to suggest?)

But many were baffling. Try reading this aloud: "An American lawyer representing women sexually abused by Jeffrey Epstein has joined forces with the family of Harry Dunn, who was killed by a car driven by Anne Sacoolas, who then fled to America claiming diplomatic immunity."

Or this: "When it was reported this week, initially in the *Financial Times*, that Nissan was considering 'doubling down' on its plant in Sunderland, pulling out of production in mainland Europe and increasing production for the UK market at its facility in the north-east, it was not only motor industry buffs who were fascinated."

If you used this sentence in a talk or presentation, would listeners be impressed?

Other opening sentences sounded OK, but their import was unclear: "The accounting watchdog is pushing ahead with an overhaul before government legislation transforms it into a more powerful body." (Was the reader meant to be furious at some kind of knavery, or delighted that the accounting watchdog was being so responsible?)

And who does "he" refer to in the following story's opening sentence: "Boris Johnson's announcement of a defining year of action on climate change was overshadowed by a former Tory energy minister's claim that he had admitted he didn't really 'get' the issue."

I guessed, as perhaps you have guessed, that the "he" referred to the Prime Minister himself, Boris Johnson. And by reading further I found that my guess was right. But careless sentences lose your reader – and your audience.

They deserve better.

One of the least glorious jobs in newspapers is rewriting other people's sentences, as a sub-editor (emphasis on sub-, not editor). I did that myself, for two or three years, a long time ago, and I'm sorry to say that, given a specimen of bad writing to improve, I didn't rejoice that I was being paid (!) to play around with sentences – perhaps improve my own writing as I did so – but grumbled, muttered and openly expressed outrage.

I have subsequently learned by experience that nobody can ensure that confusing and bad sentences don't appear in newspapers that are written, printed and distributed fast. This has not stopped me wanting to buy and read newspapers. And it is only in order to help you that I suggest some ways sub-editors might have improved the opening sentences I just quoted – if they'd had a bit more time, and had read them aloud.

The front-page lead, which packed too much into the first sentence, could perhaps focus on a single idea: "Eleven thousand women have been called in for checks after the surgeon who treated them was jailed for maiming patients."

The legal story could be simpler too: "A celebrated American lawyer is pursuing the fugitive diplomat who killed a British teenager in a car accident." (The fact that this lawyer is also involved in a high-profile sex-abuse case is too much to burden readers with in one sentence.)

Motoring story: "Nissan is investing in Sunderland and ceasing production in mainland Europe, confounding expectations that it would pull out of the UK."

Environment: "A former Tory energy minister says Boris Johnson 'doesn't get' climate change."

In each case, I tried to improve the sentences by making them shorter and clearer. This is something that works well in newspapers, and it's a useful skill in life generally. Short sentences, whether you memorise them or read from a script, are easier to put across.

But short and simple is not the only way to be interesting. Far from it. Here's the long opening sentence from a novel (*A Heart So White*, by Javier Marías, translated by Margaret Jull Costa):

"I did not want to know but I have since come to know that one of the girls, when she wasn't a girl any more and hadn't long been back from her honeymoon, went into the bathroom, stood in front of the mirror, unbuttoned her blouse, took off her bra and aimed her own father's gun at her heart, her father at the time was in the dining room with other members of the family and three guests."

Few speeches and presentations open with a stunning opening sentence because – rightly – we begin with expressions of thanks for being invited, important information about fire alarms, toilets and the timing of the next coffee break. But eventually "The Speech" begins. And it's here that you might want to serve up something special. So practise, and learn from others!

Here are some more opening sentences, by authors I admire, which I've taken at random from books on my shelf (one of them, from an anthology of journalism, restores the reputation of newspaper prose). Reading these, I find myself compelled to read on. What about you? Read them aloud, savouring the taste of every word.

"He did not, he said, remember the occasion of his parents' death, having been at the time only five months old." – William Trevor

"After a light lunch last Wednesday, General James F Hollingworth, of Big Red One, took off in his helicopter and killed more Vietnamese than all the troops he commanded." – Nicholas Tomalin, *The Sunday Times*

"Miss Brooke had that kind of beauty which seems to be thrown into relief by poor dress." – George Eliot

"It must be, Ruth thought, that she was going to die in the spring." – Lorrie Moore

"I am obliged to begin this story with a brief account of the Hampton family, because it is necessary to emphasise the fact, once and for all, that the Hamptons were very grand as well as very rich." – Nancy Mitford

"I have so far released for publication only one episode from uncle Oswald's diaries." – Roald Dahl

As well as looking at these opening lines, and even thinking about why you like them, why not use them as a model for a sentence about whatever's on your mind right now. You may not come up with anything worthy of William Trevor, George Eliot or Lorrie Moore – but nobody expects that. Just enjoy yourself as you practise an important skill.

To show you what I mean, I'll do it myself. Here's the first, by William Trevor, as applied to A Certain Person in my family (semi-fictional):

She didn't, she said, know how the glass got broken because she always hid in the loo when it was time to wash the dishes.

Here's the Tomalin, applied to something even more personal:

After a massive bowl of soup last night, Mr John-Paul Flintoff, a resident of north London, took a cross-legged position on the floor of his living room and spent more time watching TV than he had spent writing in the library all week.

You get the idea.

I wrote these very fast, changing the original as little as necessary. The point of the exercise is to internalise the rhetorical structure rather than to create a heartbreaking work of staggering genius (to quote Dave Eggers).

This is how writers learn to be great writers. After he finished playing his friend the author Hunter S Thompson, in film, the actor Johnny Depp told a journalist: "You know Hunter typed *The Great Gatsby*? He'd look at each page [F Scott] Fitzgerald wrote, and he copied it. The entire book. And more than once. Because he wanted to know what it felt like to write a masterpiece."

Thompson started doing this in the late 1950s, when he worked as a copy boy at *Time* magazine. He also typed out Hemingway's *A Farewell to Arms*, and some stories by Faulkner.

Surely, the least you can do is copy out a few sentences. And while you're at it, some first sentences from speeches you admire.

If you're thinking, "I don't know any!", I suggest you look for some online. You might also buy a book of great speeches, perhaps even subscribe to *Vital Speeches of the Day*, which has published good ones, in full, every month since 1934.

## Rhetoric is...

A few paragraphs back, I mentioned rhetoric. Sorry about that. But also: not sorry. Stanley Baldwin, Churchill's predecessor as Prime Minister, pronounced himself suspicious of rhetoric. He said that "truth needs no art at all".

But that's silly. If you try to write a sentence artlessly – well, I don't know how you can do that. Not unless you're off your head on booze and drugs. Everything we say is rhetoric: the Greeks who first classified figures of thought and figures of speech didn't invent sneaky new forms of discourse, they just zipped around the place taking note of what seemed to work and what didn't, then popped labels on the various categories.

We've already seen that people can get bored easily, and I've explained how badly built sentences confuse and alienate readers and listeners. Your own experience probably confirms that you are more likely to be bored when no art has been applied than otherwise. Even the sound of a speech can put us to sleep, if it's flatly unmusical.

But there's no point my pretending that rhetoric is a neutral idea: for good reasons it has acquired a bad name. Perhaps that could change? It does seem remarkable that a skill once considered indispensable has come to be regarded as the mastery of deceit, perhaps even immoral.

Puzzling over this conundrum with my pencil the other day, I made a list, headed "Rhetoric is..."

– the water we swim in – a means of control – a taxonomic system, endlessly divisible – something Plato distrusted – a matter of Ethos, Logos and Pathos – what modern online marketers use – fascinating – the enemy of logic – what St

Jerome feared would take him to hell – a Greek word – a means to discover the truth – divisible into Attic (plain), Ciceronian (middle) and Asiatic (high) style – a discipline to master – an art to enjoy – better than fighting with bare knuckles – a tool of democracy and law – unavoidable if you use language – a means to be dishonest – a word that has become pejorative – something Churchill used well – something Hitler (mis)used well – invaluable – the key to progress – "To be or not to be?" and everything else in Shakespeare

The list is not exhaustive, and I'm sure you can think of things I've missed. But what I concluded after drawing up this list was that rhetoric is, in itself, neutral. What really matters is the use to which you put it. It's a tool. To hate rhetoric is like hating a frying pan, just because it is possible to hit somebody on the head with one.

## Figures of thought

As a classification system for achieving verbal effects, rhetoric includes terminology from Greek, Latin and other languages, plus jargon that is tremendously up to date and (therefore) may soon become outdated.

One term that I've seen or heard a lot recently is "humblebrag", used to describe a way of showing off while seeming to be bashful. It's used especially about individuals addressing the world through social media: "Little could I have imagined that today the Nobel committee would invent a new prize just for little me" – that kind of thing.

In passing: the term humblebrag is itself a specimen of oxymoron (the rhetorical term for something that combines opposites), and a neologism (a new word), and falls into other categories too, because for historical reasons the classification system is a bit of a muddle. If you felt like it, you could waste an entire lifetime arguing about terminology, just as you could argue over the correct classification of hammers and screwdrivers, instead of devoting your life more happily to turning screws and banging nails.

So, what kind of screws do you wish to turn, and how big are the nails you are bashing? Oh, by the way, the previous two sentences were brought to you courtesy of analogy. Analogy is a rhetorical figure used to refine an idea. It's a figure of thought. Figures of speech, on the other hand, are generally used to make something sound good. In reality, any figure you use will necessarily affect both the idea you express and its music. You will recall that Erasmus, to demonstrate variety, devised dozens of ways to say he was pleased to receive a letter. While similar, each one has a slightly different effect.

The rhetorical figures available to you, which you have probably been using all your life, whether you know their names or not, will help you to perform the following tasks: refine ideas; achieve balance, clarity, emphasis or restatement; transition to a new phase; speed things up or slow them down; add playfulness, music and drama.

(Cor blimey, what a toolbox.)

While writing this book, I read a lot about rhetoric and fell in love all over again with the way words work. I can't remember being so excited about it since I was at university, studying the great poets. One of the books I enjoyed recently was Mark Forsyth's *The Elements of Eloquence*, in which he walks his readers through a variety of figures, lobbing in great examples as he goes.

I copied down many of these, then also had a go at writing my own versions, much as I did with the opening sentences quoted above. I strongly encourage you to do the same. Not only because you have a talk or presentation coming up but also because it can be delightful to create something new for its own sake.

Having finished Forsyth's book, I sat down one Saturday morning after breakfast and used many of the figures he mentions for a single purpose: to develop my thinking on the idea I mentioned at the start of this book, that the best speakers stay away from the twin extremes of a) crowd-pleasing and b) indifference to their audience. I wondered if writing the idea out, in a variety of figures, would help me to understand it better, as well as making it easier for me to express my understanding to others.

It did. I recommend you try something similar.

## Visuals

When Brian Jenner, the speechwriter who used to advertise in the back of *Private Eye*, invited me to his conference of speechwriters in Paris last year, I was pleased to see that the guests included Max Atkinson, formerly speechwriter to the Liberal Democrat leader Paddy Ashdown. Atkinson is celebrated for taking a woman with no previous experience of public speaking and training her, on a TV programme, with great success, to speak at a party conference.

In his thoroughly practical book, *Lend Me Your Ears*, Atkinson points out how odd it is that the people he works with, who are often fiercely critical of others who use boring PowerPoint slides in their presentations, frequently use the same dreary slides in their own. Very reasonably, he asks: "Why is it that so many people continue to aspire to a style of speaking that fails to impress or inspire them when they are on the receiving end?"

What people particularly object to about slide presentations is that the slides are usually full of text that is hard to read, and Very Boring Indeed to look at, and that the speaker tends to look at the slides rather than engage with the audience.

This is not the worst that can be said about PowerPoint. The most devastating critique was probably the one put together by Edward Tufte, professor emeritus at Yale and an expert in data presentation.

After the space shuttle Columbia burned up in re-entry, Nasa engaged Tufte to investigate the presentations that were used internally to assess the risk to Columbia after it was hit by foam during take-off. His forensic analysis demonstrated that PowerPoint is structurally incapable of the nuance required, and it's hard not to conclude, after reading his report, that the tragedy might have been avoided if the analysts hadn't used it.

Your own presentation may not have quite such high stakes. But every presenter wants to be understood, and get a point across. So there are several things you need to consider. One is that nobody wants you to read what they can read for themselves. So keep text to a minimum.

Data, however, is often much better understood visually than verbally. Do I mean pie charts, line graphs and bar charts? They have their place, but you could do so much better. I recommend that, like Nasa, you turn to Tufte.

In a magazine interview, Tufte said: "Sometimes displays of evidence have, as a by-product, extraordinary beauty: aesthetic or pretty, but also amazing, wonderful, powerful, never seen before... If statistics are boring, then you've got the wrong numbers. Inspired design can cause the 'right' numbers to flash out from the statistical murk."

When I first saw his masterpiece, *The Visual Display of Quantitative Information*, I couldn't believe that the options for displaying data could be so various. In the book, he includes his own ideas, as well as ideas from others. It made me laugh aloud when I came across what I'd never seen before, on page 142: Chernoff Faces.

As the name suggests, these present data in the form of a face. They're named after the academic who first devised them, Herman Chernoff. Individual parts, such as head shape, eyes, nose, ears, and their placement and orientation, are varied to reflect particular data. The idea behind this is that humans recognise faces and notice small differences easily.

At the time, I was working at the *Financial Times* magazine, and I desperately wanted to put Chernoff Faces in it. But how? The first opportunity was the Final of the FA Cup, contested that year between Arsenal and Liverpool. Taking data from the football season then reaching its conclusion, I was able to design faces with (among other statistical-facial correlations) larger noses for prolific goalscorers (who can sniff opportunities), wider eyes for those who made the most successful passes, and eyebrows that ranged from lofty angelic innocence to deepset diabolical fury to reflect player's disciplinary record. Arsenal's players had yellow faces, Liverpool's were red, for reasons that don't need spelling out if you know anything about football, and won't care to learn if you don't.

My editor, a man of considerable wisdom, happened to be lacking a decent centre spread that week and recognised a good thing when he saw it. The faces went in.

In his book, Tufte says the Chernoff Face will "reduce well, maintaining legibility even with individual areas of 0.05 square inches... We would appear to have reached the limit of graphical economy of presentation, imagination, and let it be admitted, eccentricity."

If you must use visuals in your talks, why not make them entertaining? I had my fun. You can have yours.

In fact, go ahead and use slides that don't have any data. Other images can also be entertaining, and there's nothing wrong with entertaining as long as you remain on-point.

You might plan an entire talk around illustrations, choosing the images first and only then writing "captions"; or you might start with the text and afterwards adorn it with pictures.

Either way, think carefully about the choreography. Too often, speakers introduce an image too early, killing the joke or insight they haven't yet delivered; or too late, making the illustration pointless.

In a book about his working life, the illustrator Quentin Blake says his preference is to illustrate a moment of tension, where something is unresolved. This avoids giving anything away too soon to readers, often children, who are tempted to flick ahead of the page they're reading.

In *Matilda*, by Roald Dahl, Blake shows the terrifying headteacher Miss Trunchbull holding up an empty plate, ready to smash over a boy's head. "This ought to seize [the new reader's] attention," he explains, "but it is still left to the author to bring the story to a climax."

In *Revolting Rhymes*, he chooses to illustrate a moment beyond the end of the story – not showing the bear eating

Goldilocks but when he has already done so: delicately wiping his mouth with a handkerchief, with girl's shoes and pigtail ribbons on the carpet at his feet.

Another thing Blake frequently does in his illustrations is add a bystander, irrelevant to the story, to signpost a mood or reaction – a smiling mouse or puzzled rabbit. A similar device is used by dramatists: a ghost, alter ego or younger self, who accompanies the main character, unseen by others, to steer the emotions of the audience.

The bystander could be you. When I first met Steve Chapman, on a Keith Johnstone training course, he played my younger self (aged sixteen) in an improvised scene that burned itself immediately onto my memory. We sat together, and Steve asked me simple questions about "his" (my) future.

All I had to do was tell him how things would work out.

He looked young, and anxious, so I wanted to reassure him that, yes, he would become a writer, yes, he would write for some prestigious newspapers, yes, he would meet amazing people, yes, he would marry and have a wonderful daughter...

All the time, I was talking about me. But what would otherwise have seemed like dreadful boasting became gentle, and (though I was astonished to realise it afterwards) touching to the moist-eyed audience.

Leaving aside the fact that we were improvisers, and that Steve was pretending to be me, aged sixteen, this is really very simple. It's essentially an onstage interview, with somebody who really cares about the answers. I'm sure that, with a bit of thought, you can imagine a way to partner with somebody and bring your presentation alive.

A few years ago, another friend, Kate Raworth, published a book called *Doughnut Economics*. In talks about it, she makes clear immediately that her ideas are not drily academic but profoundly about human beings. And when she started doing those talks, I was lucky enough to witness her brainstorming ways to enliven what could so easily be dull. One delightful idea was to eliminate boring line graphs. Instead, Kate would take brightly coloured ropes on stage and call for volunteers to hold the ropes, variously high and low as she directed them – a kind of living, breathing "human graph". In their own way, the volunteers incidentally would become something like Blake's smiling mice and puzzled rabbits, because they can hardly help showing on their faces the feeling that her graph conveys. Deservedly, *Doughnut Economics* became a best-seller.

As with everything else, the use of props depends on the particular situation, and what you want to achieve. Novelty for its own sake isn't pleasing on all occasions (at a funeral, for instance).

## Showing the video

Back to Mexico. I decided to improvise my talk. I had two ideas.

Standing backstage and sitting in the audience, I had watched many people from outside Mexico come on stage and say interesting things. But I hadn't seen any Mexicans talking. (They may have been there, but I missed them.) I wanted to do something that involved getting some Mexicans on stage.

As well as that I had the video – the terrible video, the video of my humiliation the previous lunchtime – which Steve encouraged me to show everybody.

I trusted him, but felt very uncomfortable. Walking backstage felt like walking towards my execution. I delivered the clip to a technician, who installed it on his laptop. I told him it was about a minute long and that I would like him to play it towards the end – but only if I gave the signal. I might get too scared to show it, I said, so please don't press "play" till I give the signal. He nodded.

And after a few other speakers, it was my turn. I walked on the vast stage, much bigger than a tennis court, and said that I had enjoyed hearing many brilliant speakers speak brilliantly. They had said many of the things I was going to say, and I wasn't sure I had much more to offer. But I felt confident, I said, looking out at this wonderful audience, that they must have some great ideas of their own.

I said how nice it might have been if some had been able to come on the stage. I said that to plant the idea in their minds, so that when, moments later, I asked for volunteers to do exactly that, they might be ready to come up at once, and not waste too many of my precious few minutes thinking about it.

I had an idea for an interactive exercise, I told them. It might be a bit chaotic. It would show them something remarkable, a helpful life lesson, but I could only do it with their help.

The game had been given to me by a fellow improviser. It's called Tigers and Horses. It's a way to demonstrate what fear looks like, and then demonstrate what courage looks like.

But I didn't say that to the audience.

Going slowly, because my words were being translated simultaneously into Spanish, I said: "What I'm going to ask you to do is very simple. You don't need to be 'good'. I just need some bodies. So can I have some volunteers?" As usual, it took a few moments for anybody to risk it, but I kept smiling, knowing that somebody in the audience wouldn't be able to take it any longer, and after the first few there would be a rush and I would have to say, OK, thank you, that's plenty!

Eventually, I had about 50 people on stage. I asked them to look around and quietly choose two other people. One of those other people is your tiger, I said. The second is your horse. Don't tell anybody who they are, but when I say the word I want you to position yourself so that your horse is between you and your tiger.

As expected, there was a bit of confusion. People wondered if they'd understood correctly. So I pointed out that every-body would have chosen different tigers and horses. You might be one person's tiger, and another person's horse. You might be everybody's tiger! But that doesn't matter. Just concentrate on your own tiger and horse, and make sure that your horse is protecting you from your tiger.

People started moving, tentatively at first then rapidly, even frantically. The group fragmented and scattered, as everybody stretched out the distance from their tigers as much as possible.

Stop! I said. Take a look around. Think about what just happened, and then I'm going to alter your instructions. They looked around, took it all in, smiled at each other.

This time, I want you to place yourself between your tiger and your horse.

They started moving, and gradually the group became tightly bunched up, a seething clump in the middle of the stage, twisting and turning as everybody sought to protect their horse.

Stop! I said again. What was the difference?

After getting a few responses, and repeating them into my microphone so that the whole audience could hear, I pointed out that the first exercise was a demonstration of fear, and the second was a demonstration of courage. When you're afraid, you scatter. When you're brave, you get stuck in.

I thanked my volunteers and gave them time to go back to their seats. But I hadn't finished, I said.

I came here to talk about how to change the world – to tell inspiring stories about people who try things that don't always work out first time, but they keep trying and eventually they succeed. I've heard lots of other people tell similar stories, and you don't need more from me. So I'm going to tell you something else.

I want to tell you that sometimes you try things and they don't work out, and it really hurts. It may get better eventually, but it may not, and until it does you have to live with that hurt. I'm going to show a video in which somebody tries something and it doesn't work out. And frankly it's embarrassing.

I gave the signal to the engineer standing offstage and the video came onto a huge screen behind me. The audience chuckled when they recognised that the man in the video was me. They chuckled more as the man in the video walked towards the hamster wheel. He stepped into the wheel, started walking, quickly assumed an anxious expression, then fell over with a loud clunk. It looked very painful. Five thousand Mexicans gasped.

Hearing that gasp, I felt mortified but also strangely comforted. They cared, and that felt good. The video stopped. I said, Well, there you are. I don't know what I was trying to do, but I didn't think it through. It was a silly mistake. Afterwards, I went back to my hotel room, feeling humiliated. I called a friend, and he said I should show you this video. That's what failure looks like. Thank you very much for your time.

As I was about to walk off, the MC – host of the entire Mexican extravaganza – bounded onstage and said, "Could we watch the video one more time?"

I couldn't imagine that my mortification could get any worse, so I said, why not?

The video restarted. This time, at the point where previously 5,000 Mexicans gasped, 5,000 Mexicans laughed. And that felt OK too.

# MEMORY

## Completely ram your mind/brain space

*A machine for remembering itself.*

Don Paterson

It's easy to forget, but for most of human history, there was no internet. Not being able to look things up any time, people made more effort in the past to use their memories, and not only for the few years at school while cramming for exams. Cultivating memory was a task – indeed, a pleasure – to last a lifetime.

Still today, people tend to be impressed by speakers who do without written notes. It's widely agreed that David Cameron won the leadership of the Conservative Party largely for that reason. We lose interest in somebody who doesn't look at us, whether they're too busy looking at sheets of paper or reading slides on a screen behind them.

Rachel Ison was determined not to do that in her

first-time speech. For days beforehand, she practised it while eating, in the bathroom getting ready for work and brushing her teeth at night. "I must've been practising for three or four days, a few times a day – and then again on the day before."

It wasn't only the exact wording she wanted to remember, she told me, but the general sequence of ideas. "I didn't want to be standing up, flustered, unable to remember the next thing to talk about. So I practised the points of each paragraph, as well as the specific words, in my head and out loud."

## Visual memory, audial memory

Does this happen to you? When I walk around in London, without meaning to do it, I often find myself remembering conversations or events that took place in the same location, even years ago. I even sometimes remember where I happened to have a particular thought, all by myself, if it was a thought that had a big impact at the time.

Sometimes I "remember" things that happened long before my birth: there's a place in Fleet Street, for instance, where Dr Johnson is reported to have stopped and laughed uncontrollably, and I always think of him when I walk there.

The connection between memory and location is strong, and the classic method of remembering, used in antiquity by people who didn't have plentiful stationery, let alone digital devices, was known as a Memory Palace. In brief: people were taught from a young age to place data, stories and ideas in imaginary locations in imaginary buildings and towns.

Recently I tried a version of this when I took a long bus journey from home. In my mind, I ran over a talk I was about to give, and attempted to link the particular insight, story or data with the world around me. Thus, the structure of the talk took the shape of that particular bus journey. The opening joke was located at the big Catholic church off Kilburn High Road. The sad story I planned to tell came at the canal near Westbourne Grove. And so on. (If you're wondering: the bus was a 328.)

The problem with my way of telling you this is that I'm doing so using words and sentences, and I always hate to be given directions in words and sentences. I can't imagine what it is like to have a brain that can cope with this kind of thing: take the third right turn, and after 250 yards there's a large building on your left, then two sets of traffic lights until you take a left, then another left, and continue for – well, you get the idea. If somebody gives me directions like these, I find myself repeating them with a kind of rehearsed movement – waving my left hand for left turns, the right hand for right turns, sometimes swivelling at the hips, because I won't remember anything without these tiny muscle memories.

It's so much easier with a map.

A modern counterpart to the memory palace is a mind map, created using a variety of pens in different colours, and a combination of words and imagery. I had never tried mind maps until I met the man who made a fortune from them, the late Tony Buzan. The School of Life invited him to speak to a large audience, and I was to be host, welcoming people and introducing him. Naturally, I bought some of his best-selling books first.

His argument for making mind maps was two-fold: the activity of drawing them helps you to understand something, and also to memorise it.

Experience has taught me that he may be right. Soon after that event, I was invited to run a three-hour class on How to Be Creative with just 24 hours' notice. Buzan's enthusiasm for mind maps was fresh in my ears, and I was inclined to believe his notion that making ideas into maps, with lots of visual detail, could be the best way to absorb them.

Over several hours, I read and re-read 15,000 words of script and notes that went into the class, making maps of it all. I made maps of the whole thing, to start with, then maps of the various individual parts of the class and maps of impro exercises that might work. Finally, as darkness fell, I made one last map, with coloured branches as Buzan recommended and little images scattered among them (ditto). One, to remind me to discuss boredom, showed a man yawning. Here is that map on the next page.

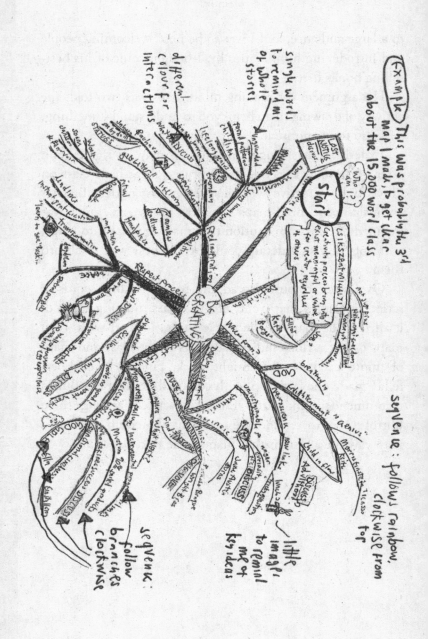

I'm happy to report that the process worked well. When the class started, I took the precaution of warning participants that I might be a bit halting, here and there, and they (therefore?) looked unbothered when I did get a couple of minor things wrong. In general, a single quick glance at that colourful map was enough to tell me where I was and where to go next – the whole point of maps, after all.

I was especially pleased that, when the class ended, people came over to ask if they could examine and admire my map, which I subsequently used many times to teach the same class, sometimes deviating from it considerably, to meet people's particular needs and interests, but always having a framework to come back to.

The late poet laureate, Ted Hughes – a friend of Buzan, as it happens – edited a selection of poetry to memorise, *By Heart*, with an introduction describing his own memory techniques, which begin visually, by mentally "photographing" the images in a poem, then gradually move to embedding the poems through sound.

Audial memory has an extraordinary capacity to hold on to sound patterns. That's why children learn songs and jingles to memorise the alphabet and multiplication tables. It's why we say, "Thirty days have September...", and we remember "I before E, except after C..."

The mnemonic phrase Richard Of York Gave Battle In Vain uses a tiny fragment of narrative to give sense to what otherwise seems bafflingly random – the colours of the rainbow. (The initial letters are the same: Red Orange Yellow Green Blue Indigo Violet.) The rhythm of the phrase also helps us to retain it, just as (I'm sure) sound explains why acronyms such as NATO, WYSIWYG and RAM help us to remember the long, stodgy abstracts they represent (The North Atlantic Treaty Organisation, What You See Is What You Get, Random Access Memory).

"The closest thing to a musical melody in a line of verse," Hughes explains, "is the pattern of sounds made by the sequence of syllables. That pattern includes rhythm and overall inflection, along with the alternation of vowels and consonants. The stronger the pattern, the more memorable the line will be."

When he was young, Hughes entered a competition to devise a catch phrase (telling term!) for Heinz beans. Following the tradition of oral poetry, using alliteration, assonance and internal rhyme, he came up with "Whoever minds how he dines demands Heinz". Not as pithy and memorable as the slogan the company adopted ("Beanz Meanz Heinz") but cunningly devised along the same principles.

"Even nonsense becomes memorable if the sound pattern is strong enough," Hughes writes. "It roots itself directly in the nerves of the ear."

Another poet, Don Paterson, says that "every device and trope, whether rhyme or metre, metaphor or anaphora, or any one of the thousand others, can be said to have a mnemonic function in addition to its structural or musical one", thus turning a poem into a machine for remembering itself. "Of all the art forms, only the poem can be carried around in the brain perfectly intact."

I'm not sure what Paterson means by art form, but the Koran, at the death of the Prophet Mohammed, was for many years only passed on orally. By the time it was eventually written down, more than 100,000 people had learned it entirely by heart. The Koran contains about 80,000 words. By learning 20 verses a day, you can memorise it in a year – and if you do, you will earn the honoured title of Hafiz.

Not bad, but what about this: Ron Boyd-MacMillan, the teacher of preachers, was once asked to devise a curriculum for a house-church movement in China. The full-time, one-year course he helped to devise was called "The 66, the 33, and the 1", because graduate students had to prepare 66 one-hour sermons, one on each book of the Bible, and learn them all by heart.; create and memorise 33 one-hour sermons on the life and work of Jesus (who died aged 33), each one based on a single verse, to cover his whole ministry, from the beginning of time, through his birth, death, resurrection, ascension and intercessory work through to the Second Coming; and finally one sermon they might preach to the patriarchs, prophets and saints at the End of Time.

If they could manage that (and, in case you are wondering, they could), perhaps we can all memorise the odd presentation without relying on PowerPoint.

## Handwriting

To help us do that, we may need to rediscover the art of writing by hand.

In an age when digital devices can accurately and quickly transcribe spoken words, it is not surprising that people resist writing by hand, and eventually stop being much good at it.

A survey in Britain recently found that one in three people had not written anything by hand for six months. Perhaps as a consequence, tests found that the average speed of copying by hand (by adults) is 68 letters per minute (roughly thirteen words). Fast writers manage 113 letters (20 words, not so bad), but slower writers copy at just 26 letters per minute (five words, ouch).

It turns out that, time-consuming though it may be, writing by hand helps us to understand information and remember it.

Some of the studies compared handwritten notes with typed notes. Typed notes tend to be verbatim. Because handwriting is slower, writers are more selective, using their brains to digest, summarise and capture what is most needed. This, in turn, promotes understanding and retention.

In memory tests afterwards, notetakers who typed performed worse, perhaps because writing by hand is known to activate more of your grey matter: tests on young children found that drawing letters activated three areas of the brain – more than typing or merely tracing the letters. Indeed, learning to write by hand seems to play an important part in learning to read (can it be done otherwise?) and drawing each letter by hand, no matter how old you are, creates a "body memory" like my waving of hands and swivelling at the hips when following directions.

Writing by hand is also more strongly linked to emotional processing than typing. This is not surprising if you remember the difference between writing something when you feel angry and writing something when you feel nervous or dizzy – the impression you make on the paper will be very different. It's been said, by experts in this area, that there is "an element of dancing" when we write, and a melody in the message that adds emotion to the text. Each person's hand is different: the gestures on paper are charged with emotion and personality.

Operating a keyboard is not the same at all. All you have to do is press the right key: the movement is the same, whatever the letter. Hunter S Thompson might have felt even more like Fitzgerald, Hemingway and Faulkner if he had written out their works by hand.

## Commonplace

A few months ago, I was prompted to start doing something I wish I had thought of long ago, when a friend told me that he was doing it. If you copy me, after reading this, then you too are indebted to him; just as he is indebted to someone else, and that person to someone before them, in a grand apostolic succession reaching back (at least) to the Renaissance, when Leonardo da Vinci described his practice of amassing "a collection without order, drawn from many papers, which I have copied here, hoping to arrange them later, each in its place, according to the subject of which they treat".

My friend, the speechwriter Brian Jenner, said he had put together a "commonplace book" at the end of last year, in time for Christmas. It would contain useful and entertaining ideas he had picked up here and there about speaking in public and writing speeches. Because I was writing this book, I asked Brian to send me a copy. A few weeks later, he did. It was no disappointment.

By this time I had learned a little more of the history and use of commonplace books, online and at the British Library. One specimen I studied there is known as "George Eliot's Blotter" – it's a two-sided writing case of blotting paper. Eliot (it turns out) was an inveterate recorder of favourite passages as well as information – always on the lookout for quotations to use as epigraphs at the start of her chapters. In the blotter, she captured verse from (among others) Tennyson, Wordsworth, Shakespeare, Goethe, Dante, Marvell, Heine, Keats, Omar Khayyam, Coleridge and Herbert.

Commonplace books were a kind of pre-digital technology for gathering things that mattered to people. Sometimes they were shared with friends or the public generally, but sharing wasn't the main point – that was to amass material and organise it in such a way that nothing was lost. Or rather (the distinction is not tiny) so that everything could easily be found.

In my excitement, I wrote a list of things that I hoped to include in my commonplace book: lists, quotes, recipes, remedies, letters, poems, measurements, proverbs, prayers, formulas, devotions, technical, documentary and literary cuttings, spreadsheets, quizzes, marketing, mind maps, question-and-answer, timelines, interviews, colours, photos, sketches, prints, manifestos, speeches, timetables, maps, rules, family trees, reviews, criticism, sermons, curses, blessings, diaries, fiction, scripts, news, feedback, glossaries, dialogue. To date, I have touched on only a very few of these. But then, I've only been collecting for a couple of months, and I have the rest of my life ahead of me, however short or long that may be.

A word about lists. Peter Mark Roget, original author of *Roget's Thesaurus*, started filling a notebook with words in 1805, sorting them by their meanings, but not publishing the first edition until 1852. It has been claimed that Roget made lists to fend off depression – list-making was then well established as a coping mechanism. And in his essay "The Crack-Up", about his breakdown, which Tazeen mentions in her TEDx talk, F Scott Fitzgerald says he resolutely tried not to think. "Instead I made lists, hundreds of lists: of cavalry leaders and football players and cities, and popular tunes and pitchers, and happy times, and hobbies and houses lived in and how many suits since I left the army and how many pairs of shoes (I didn't count the suit I bought in Sorrento that shrunk, nor the pumps and dress shirt and collar that I carried around for years and never wore, because the pumps got damp and grainy and the shirt and collar got yellow and starch-rotted). And lists of women I'd liked, and of the times

I had let myself be snubbed by people who had not been my betters in character or ability."

A list of lists by a man with depression.

You've already read how useful Tazeen found it to write things down.

If you don't happen to have dissociative amnesia, or feel depressed, you may consider it unnecessary to write things down, because we live in an age when virtually any fact or opinion can be found online. Please, think again! If you do only that, you leave no trace of what you yourself have learned, and what you care about, to pick up and enjoy again later. And if you don't remember a particular insight, did you ever really learn it?

This week, I read the obituary of the polymath and academic George Steiner. It quoted him saying that most modern teaching is "organised amnesia", because it takes away the art of remembrance. Steiner urged his students to "put luggage inside you so that when the wind starts blowing you have ballast".

Recently I threw away notebooks containing notes from twelve years of interviews as a journalist. Twelve! It was painful, but I couldn't see the point in keeping them: I had never looked at any of them, because they were written in shorthand, and though I can still read shorthand easily enough when I apply myself, it has never leapt out of the page like normal text. I can't quickly scan a page of shorthand to find a key word – so I have never bothered. Because there was no organising principle to help me find things afterwards, and because I will never have time to read every page I wrote over twelve years, the notebooks were useless.

In researching commonplace books online, I discovered simple techniques that could have helped me "tag" hand-written content and locate it by volume, page and date. To start, leave two pages blank at the front, to fill in as a "contents" page whenever you write in the book, and add the relevant page numbers. At the back, create an index of general topic areas. Assign a different colour to each one. In my own book, any entry that has to do with oratory is marked with orange pen on the edge of the page. Other topics have other colours. Flicking through the book, I can quickly find material on any particular theme by looking for pages marked with the relevant colour. And if I know already the specific passage I'm looking for, I can simply scan the index to find the page. When you finish one book, before you start another, type out your contents page and save a digital copy.

Looking back, I can think of many things that I would have liked to put into a commonplace book, if only I had started earlier.

When I was working on the *Financial Times* magazine, I walked out of the office one lunchtime with John Lloyd, a senior journalist who had once been a correspondent in Soviet Russia. I don't remember where we were going, but I do remember something he told me about his Russian experience. (And I remember the exact stretch of pavement where we were walking as he told me.) Someone he met, perhaps interviewed, once showed him Stalin's personal copy of Machiavelli's book, *The Prince*. I think John said the book had been annotated. He didn't remember specifics. This (if I were able to read Russian) would be a remarkable thing to take down in a commonplace book: the specific lines that Stalin underscored, and the marginal notes he wrote.

I've since started a new notebook with pages devoted to specific figures of thought and speech. If I come across a good one, I pop it in. I'm convinced that the fruits of great minds might eventually yield seeds in my own (metaphor).

You might agree that collecting words in a commonplace book is helpful to writers. But is it also useful to people who speak?

It is. (This one-person Q&A is an example of prolepsis, the rhetorical figure by which the speaker pre-empts likely objections with a question, then immediately provides an answer. Now, let's get back to what I was saying.)

It is.

There are too many examples to choose from, but once again Winston Churchill provides a good case. I have already explained that Churchill took a very long time preparing his speeches. During the war, as Prime Minister, he simply couldn't give them quite as much time as he might have otherwise. Happily for him, he had collected plenty of material by that point in his life, including an enormous bank of metaphors, similes and other rhetorical devices. Indeed, several of the phrases for which he is now best remembered had been used on other occasions, often long before the war started – and thus were readily available for him to draw on in his (sorry!) finest hour.

### Interlude: a personal story

Alas, you can't be prepared for everything. A few years ago, a succession of both major and minor traumas hit me. Double bereavement. Serious health scares involving people close to me. A change in direction at The School of Life, which meant I could no longer work there. I had no contract with a newspaper, nor anybody else giving me regular work. Each one of these might have been manageable on its own, but together they hurt me. And for reasons I didn't understand, they brought back memories of difficult times from long ago. I became depressed.

But I didn't tell anybody. And as my confidence declined, I got less work, causing me to worry about money, which in turn affected my work.

Someone asked me to give a talk to his business network in Oxford. I agreed, partly because he was a friend, but also because even the small fee he offered was better than nothing.

At his request, I wrote something to drum up interest and sent it off. Then I heard nothing, but that was quite normal – everyone is busy.

As the date of my talk approached, I chased up to see if there was more I could do. No reply.

But I booked a train ticket, and let him know I was looking forward to it. Still I heard nothing. Two days beforehand, I got a message saying that only one person had booked, and the talk was cancelled. I have no idea how much activity went into promoting it. But I was left with the lingering, nagging feeling that people stayed away because it was me.

Again, I didn't say this to anyone. Probably a big mistake. As Brené Brown had already told me, shame thrives on secrecy – and could probably have been dispelled quickly if I had told someone.

Determined that what had (not) happened in Oxford

should never (not) happen again, I looked online for help – clearly, I had to up my game – and soon fell prey to the modern counterparts of the Sophists, those Greeks who taught rhetoric to anyone who could afford their fees.

Being desperate, I was a perfect target for the self-styled "gurus of online marketing". I started watching the free videos in which they explained some of their techniques. The first video always contained surprising ideas and tantalising promises, making it very easy to watch the second. In the second video, they provided still more entertainment and real, useful, practical tips, with the promise of even more wonderful things in the third video – and a cautionary aside to the effect that nothing I had learned so far would work properly unless I kept watching all the way to the end. So I watched the third video, and at the end of that my new virtual friend and mentor made me an offer: if I paid a certain amount – much less than the normal price, he assured me, and it was always a he – I could become a true master, and move my business onto a sound financial foundation.

The first few times, of course, I didn't pay. Instead, I abandoned that particular guru and started looking for a new one, who might let slip the Big Secret. Each one was able to reveal the tremendous effect of their guidance on clients who had become very rich and successful after following their advice. And they were delightfully open about how the techniques they were using on me – such as withholding key bits of information till the end and only sharing it with paying customers – would in turn help me to do that to my own customers, causing me too to become very rich and successful.

Suddenly, I was paying hundreds of pounds online to someone I'd never heard of a day earlier. Later, seeking more and more of this wisdom, I would pay thousands of pounds. And the fact that had I paid so much, so quickly, was wonderful: this man could help me get money out of my own clients because – behold! – he had got money out of me. He knew what he was talking about. I was myself living proof. Sure, his manner was a bit full-on, a bit hard-sell, but I put that down to him being American. That's probably normal, where he's from. And perhaps it should be normal where I'm from. It's probably where I've been going wrong. I should be more full-on and hard-sell myself. But how?

I had so much to learn.

As I tried to put the gurus' lessons into practice, I abandoned my instincts, my ideas, my way of expressing myself, in an effort to be somebody else – somebody better. I didn't do anything absolutely demonic, but it wasn't right. One day, I sent an email to a group of people and one of them sent a gentle reply asking if I had really meant to send it to her. Another day, responding to something else, another woman asked if I was feeling OK.

Meanwhile, back in the real world... in a corporate training session, half of the 50 or so participants walked out on me. Then I talked to 700 girls in a secondary school, only to be told the next day, in an email, that I had caused terrible offence.

I was devastated. I couldn't understand exactly how I'd done it, and I wasn't given the chance to put things right.

I concluded that I was profoundly useless – beyond hope.

Now, I'm fairly sure you didn't start reading this book

to learn that a few speaking events going badly would make a hitherto adequate speaker admit himself to psychiatric hospital, where, to his own considerable surprise, he was placed on what nobody officially terms suicide watch. You were hoping for something more motivating than that.

But hang on. Were you not paying attention when I told you, earlier, that Cicero – that all-time master of oratory – paid with his life for a speech that was misjudged? The hand that wrote it was cut off, and the wife of the person he offended stuck pins in the dead orator's tongue.

But don't worry. It's unlikely to happen to you. And that's a motivating thought, if ever there was one.

You didn't expect, I daresay, when you started reading, that you would hear about the author being put on suicide watch. But a willingness to be candid is fundamental to speaking and presenting. Speeches aren't delivered in a pristine, parallel world where everything is easy. I wish they were, but they're not.

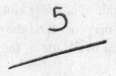

# DELIVERY

### Give a super presentation

*Nothing will ever be attempted, if all possible objections must first be overcome.*

Samuel Johnson

## The big moment

The first people to arrive at Ison's house were her cousins, so mercifully there was no expectation to perform. Then others came, enough to chat among themselves. "They knew about the charity, and they knew it was a fundraising tea, because I'd sent an email with a couple of sentences about it. Some people asked questions about the charity, understandably, but I didn't want to go into my speech early, so I said, 'I'm going to stand up and say something properly in an hour or so.'"

She'd planned to say something at 4.30, and as the time approached she withdrew into the garage, where it was quiet, to read her speech one last time. "I put it on top of the recycling bin, which is kind of eye level for me. I read it out loud a few times. Probably panicked a bit. Then my mum came in and said, 'Oh, I was looking for you, are you OK?' 'Yeah, just, just nervous.' And she goes, 'OK, let's do it. There's a good amount of people in the room.' 'OK,' I said. 'Let's do it.'

"I think when I walked into the room, someone had already rounded people up, but I can't actually remember. I got into position. And I remember feeling hot, really hot – like, neck heat. And I just started. I think I was... I mean I don't know how it sounded to anyone else, but I felt like my voice was a bit shaky when I said my first few words, because I was really nervous.

"I had my notes in my hand, but down against my lap so I could see them. No one else could see them, but they were there. And after the first 30 seconds or a minute I was in my stride. I'd said this many times before. I relaxed."

She knew that it's a good idea to make eye contact around the room. "So I remember really consciously looking around the room at different people. But I didn't want to look at my mum, and luckily she wasn't directly ahead of me, 'cause I thought she would probably be crying, especially at the end."

A friend's baby made muffled sounds throughout, without being disruptive. "But then as I was moving from one paragraph to the next, he made a really loud cry and it threw me off. I didn't make a thing of it. I acknowledged the baby in a nice way, then carried on. And I was relieved that the flow continued. It hadn't thrown me off long — it felt like ages, but can't have been more than two seconds.

"I can't remember exactly what I said at the end, but it was something along the lines of 'People who no longer feel life is worth living don't necessarily want to die, but they don't want to carry on living the life they have'. That was the last thing I said before I said thank you."

She never directly requested funding, but thanked everyone who had supported the charity so far, and said that if anyone would like to contribute, they still could. She'd expected to raise a thousand pounds, but surpassed that severalfold.

Only after finishing did she glance at her mother, who was not crying but looked proud ("which was nice"). Then several individuals approached to talk to her one-to-one, a few of them in tears. "They wanted to know how they could volunteer, which was probably the best outcome of all, because it's a completely volunteer-run charity. For people to have been inspired by what I told them, inspired enough to say, 'Oh, I'd really like to do that, it sounds really meaningful' — that was great."

## First lines

Ison was very sensible to invite a friendly audience to her first public speech. It reduced the pressure to look "good", which other speakers feel intensely from the very beginning.

This is why a good opening sentence helps. But a powerful opening in a speech is not the same as the first sentence in a book or newspaper. It's not fixed, though audiences often assume it is. Being live, it's changeable – and you can play on the audience's assumption. Allow me to give you an example.

When giving talks about my previous book, I used to start by saying, "If you had the chance, would you change the world?" At first, this question was intended as erotesis (a rhetorical question that implies a strong affirmation and doesn't bother to wait for it). Over time, doing the same talk again and again, I discovered entirely by chance that by leaving the question in the air for a moment I could flush out the audience. Like this:

"If you had the chance, would you change the world?"

Silence.

I let the silence sink in for a moment and said, "Oh, dear!"

Then I asked the question again.

This time, a few people – sometimes many people –would shout out, "Yes!"

To which I was able to reply, "Good. Because you can. And I'm here to tell you how." What I had done was achieve a kind of "buy in" at the beginning, which made everything afterwards so much easier.

By asking a question and being willing to wait for an answer, I discovered that I could allow an audience to recognise that they were not passive consumers but participants, active agents – which was the point, after all, of my talk.

In a book, I can urge and cajole you as much as I like but

will never know your response. I'll never know if you had a go at writing out your own version of rhetorical figures. In a live event, with real people, the response is obvious and immediate, even when it's a long silence. A long silence is what most of us are afraid of. It feels terribly risky – what if nobody says anything!? And regrettably few speakers take that risk. Let's see if we can change that.

(Eh? What did you say? I can't hear you!)

## Dare to do it differently

It's nearly 20 years since I first met Brendan Barns. I was writing for the *Financial Times* magazine at the time. He had a crazy dream: to make business conferences not-boring. To write about this, I followed him around for weeks as he remortgaged his home and risked everything for his launch event, hiring the BBC presenter John Humphrys as MC and the globally renowned management writer Charles Handy as his main speaker. Oh, and an orchestra to get things started with oomf.

As a writer, I found Brendan delightful and good value because he was so candid, and the stakes were high: "It's not easy," he said when we first met before his face resumed its resting expression of bottomless anxiety. "This is a massive personal cost – half a million pounds, and I can't afford that unless we get the right number of delegates. We have six weeks to get another 200 people. Worst-case scenario? I lose my home. Do I have sleepless nights? I do."

Since then, he's managed to keep his home and the business has flourished. He'll soon have put on more than 400 of his corporate entertainments. There's no reason why that should stop, he says, because most rival business events continue to be places where most people go to lose the will to live.

"Some people who are asked to go to a business conference think it's a punishment. They say, 'Why me? Can't someone else go?'" he said.

I ask Brendan to tell me, what, from his experience, makes a good speaker.

"My view is that any speaker at any level in any sector should think about how best to inspire their audience, whether it's an internal meeting or a conference with lots of clients and potential clients, because the audience genuinely wants to enjoy whatever it is they're given."

Many speakers, even after preparing a talk well, mess it up as soon as they begin, Brendan says. "An example of that is when you go to an event and somebody comes on stage and says, 'I've got to give you the boring stuff, you know, about the fire exit, and what to do if the alarm goes off.' This sets off the expectation that the speaker is going to be boring. Why?! Information about what you need to do in the event of a fire can be done in a fun way. You just have to look at things a bit differently. People want to have a good time. People learn more when the information is presented in an engaging way. So don't handicap yourself by saying 'I've got boring information for you'. No! If the information is boring, make it interesting. You don't read stories to your children and pre-empt it by saying, 'This is going to be a really boring story.' Use some imagination!"

I point out that some people truly believe that the thing

they are talking about is boring. They think that they themselves are boring.

"I realise that some people are technical experts. And if you're an expert in widgets, you might think, well, I'm a bit of a geek, and this information can't be made interesting. I disagree! I don't care what the subject is. I don't care what your technical expertise is. I believe anything can be presented in an inspiring and engaging way by daring to have some imagination. Dare to do it a bit differently. Suddenly, you will break down your audience. They'll look at you and think, this guy's human. We thought he was some kind of technical machine. But actually he can engage, and create rapport, and tell stories. That's what great speakers do, but anybody can do it."

## Talk to the dandelions

Steve Chapman, who launched his book by busking, used to work as an executive coach. His clients included many people who either were boring, or thought they were. So Steve gave them what he called Creative Adventures.

One man wanted to learn to be more free and spontaneous. He was a senior executive, vice president of finance (or similar) in a pharmaceutical organisation. And in this eminent position he received feedback telling him that the polished professionalism that had got him there no longer worked in his favour. "His team were saying he didn't seem very human," Steve said. "He seemed very... well, just not inspiring."

They met for the first time in a coffee shop inside the

vast offices where the man worked. The man described his problem. Steve recalls: "I thought, 'This is do or die.' I could say, 'Go away and think if you want to work with me.' Or we could just do something. If he wants to experience 'exciting and spontaneous', then let's do something exciting and spontaneous. So I said, let's go for a walk."

They got up, walked outside onto the heathland opposite the company's headquarters. "He was talking: blah, blah, blah, blah... And I thought, yeah, you are quite dull!"

Then Steve saw a clump of dandelions and said, "Tell the dandelions your vision for your department."

The executive didn't understand. He said, "What?"

"And I said, 'No, do it! The dandelions – they're all gathered here, today, to hear you do your speech. Can you do it?'"

Steve had no idea what he was doing. It was a spontaneous suggestion, and felt scary for him too. To his relief, the man started a talk about his vision for the finance department.

"And I thought, if I was a dandelion, I wouldn't have a clue what's going on. So I got down and held the dandelions, and moved them about, saying in a dandelion voice, 'We don't understand!' Then I said, in my own voice, 'I don't understand. You're gonna have to change it.' I could tell he was getting frustrated – angry, even – and wondering, what's the point in all this? But he kept going. And then he started talking about fiscal growth.

"And at that point I just started playing. 'We don't care about fiscal growth, we're dandelions!' He got so frustrated."

It wasn't calculated. Steve just did it. But with hindsight, he realised this was what Zen Masters do: frustrate people, to make them try something new.

"At one point, I got two dandelions, made them turn to face each other and say, 'I don't know what this is about. Should we go?' And then my client laughed. And in that moment, it was like, 'Ah, I see you now! That's you!' And all the dandelions went, 'Yeeeeaaaah! There he is!'"

Steve mentioned a story in Oliver Burkeman's book, *The Antidote*. One of the people Burkeman interviewed suggested he try something bold – shout out the names of the stations, travelling on London Underground, moments before the automated announcer said them. "So he'd be travelling on the Central Line and shout out, 'Holborn!', or whatever," Steve said. "And of course, he was worried that everyone would look at him, but he found there came a point where the anticipated experience and the actual experience crossed over, and it was no longer as bad as he might have expected. It was like that for my client, with the dandelions. He let go, and it was totally liberating."

Unless you are willing to let go, you won't take risks. Take no risks, and you'll get bored. Get bored, and you'll bore others. Bore others, and you'll lose the things that, for fear of losing them, make you too scared to take risks.

## Arrogant twat

A few years ago, I took a small risk running a workshop on confidence at The School of Life. At the very beginning, after giving my name but saying nothing else, I said to the group in front of me, "You've come to the right person because I've given this subject a lot of thought."

That's all. As I said it, I was aiming for cheerful self-confidence, nothing else. Then I said, "OK. Time out. Pause."

And then I asked, "I want to know what you think of the person who just said what I said. What was the impact of that sentence on you?"

It took a long time for anyone to come out with an answer – after all, this was a room full of people who had come to a session on how to be confident. But with a bit of encouragement, one person put her hand up, then another. I seem to remember it was only women, at first anyway. (The class was mostly made up of women: more confident than men about turning up to a class to learn confidence.) Most said that hearing me say it felt good: they were pleased they weren't wasting their money, or words to that effect.

Naturally I was happy that they said that, but I tried not to get too attached to it because that wasn't the point. (This was well before my breakdown.)

Some people hadn't spoken, and I added, "I'm sure there must be someone else who thinks something different –even slightly different." And I kept on giving reassurances that whatever they wanted to say was fine, it was all interesting, all useful for an exercise that we were doing.

Eventually the first man put his hand up. I said, "Oh great! What did you think?"

He was a bit cautious about how he said it, but eventually he came out with it: "Well, when you said that, I thought you were a bit of an arrogant twat."

I was so pleased. Not because I want people to think I'm an arrogant twat, but because it demonstrated what I'd hoped to demonstrate: all these people had seen exactly the same person say exactly the same thing, and between them they'd had slightly (or significantly) different responses to him.

It wasn't me that was different – it was them.

Why emphasise this point? Because it meant that I couldn't control what other people think of me. So I could stop trying. Not even bother. Just be myself and get on with it. I was free. I had tasted the very essence of confidence. I told them that, then proceeded with the class as usual.

Sadly, that freedom doesn't last, because unless you are a psychopath, you do care what people think, and you are likely to forget that you can't control what other people think of you.

If you aren't yet convinced that you can't, let me tell you about another experiment.

This time, I was running an impro workshop in a prison, with long-term sex offenders, as it happens, but the results were identical to the results I had when I worked with management consultants. (Make of that what you will.)

It had taken a long time to warm up the participants, because while they didn't care what I thought about them, they certainly didn't want to look stupid in front of each other, because they would be stuck together for years. Eventually, a few bolder inmates volunteered to do the odd demonstration: very simple things to begin with, which they pulled off well, winning applause, so gradually I increased the riskiness of what I asked them to do. It looked bold, and they were rewarded with louder applause. Soon enough they were finding it exhilarating, and leaping up to volunteer before anybody else did.

At this point I said, "Let's pretend you're at a party." Four volunteers pretended to be at a party. It didn't look like the most amazing party, but they were enjoying themselves.

I said, "OK, let's do it again, but with a twist." (Once again, I owe this exercise entirely to Keith Johnstone.) This time, I whispered a personal characteristic to each of the four. I asked one to be the "funny" party guest. One would be the "gloomy" guest. Another would be "sexy" and the last one "bashful". I told the audience that the volunteers would be doing the same party scene but each one with a particular characteristic, and they had to guess at the end who was what.

They did more or less the same as before, but this time the funny one told jokes and laughed at them. The sexy one looked into an imaginary mirror with evident pleasure. I don't recall exactly what the bashful and gloomy ones did. But afterwards when I asked the audience to guess each man's secret, nobody got it right. They thought the gloomy one was "boring". They thought the sexy one was "vain". The funny one was "arrogant".

So far as it went, this was as I had expected. "It's extremely hard to make other people see you in a particular way," I said, as if this was some absolutely stunning revelation instead of something we all experience every day.

"Let's try it with a different twist."

This time, the instructions were given openly to them all, and the audience heard too. "I want you to look at each other. Without telling anybody which is which, I want you to decide that one of the other three on stage with you is really funny. Another is sexy. And the third has a reputation for violence."

I went on to spell out what might otherwise have been confusing. "You might not choose the same 'funny' person as anyone else. That doesn't matter. You may find that everybody has chosen the same person to be potentially violent. It might be you! That doesn't matter either. Just remember who you have decided is funny, sexy and violent, and behave towards them accordingly."

They played the scene again, and it was terrifically funny. Everybody could see instantly that person X seemed funny to person Y, because even the most boring comment from X provoked loud laughter. It was immediately obvious who was deemed sexy or violent because people moved chairs closer to them, or further away, respectively. One man had been chosen as "violent" by two others, and it was hard for anybody watching not to see him in that light too. The characteristic had more effectively been "endowed" on him by others than stimulated by the man himself.

It was like a living, breathing equivalent of what Quentin Blake achieves with the mice in his illustrations: an onlooker can guide, by means of a smile or a frown, how the viewer understands a scene; can make other people funny by laughing at their comments, or menacing by backing away from them.

Let's slow down and consider what this means.

Our assumptions colour the way we see others.

Other people's assumptions colour the way they see us.

At the start of this book, I raised the notion that an audience might hate (say) British people. More recently, I described a man who thought I was an arrogant twat. It's painful to consider that people might take against us.

And I've tried to demonstrate that you can't control what anybody thinks of you.

The good news is that, while we can't control what others think of us, we can change what we think of them.

And by some kind of magic, that sometimes changes what they think of us.

(Results not guaranteed.)

When Keith was teaching this, he followed up with another experiment. He asked for seven volunteers, whom he lined up in front of the rest of us.

"This is a group of world-famous Colombian jugglers," he told us. The improvisers, talented though they were, exchanged nervous glances. "All I want you to do is enter the room and take the applause before you amaze us with your juggling."

There were more nervous glances. "Don't worry, you don't need to juggle, just take the applause." The seven walked out of the room. Keith said, "Oh, hang on, I've forgotten something", and went after them. And after a moment he returned, with instructions for the rest of us: the jugglers' audience.

"I want you to give them a really fantastic welcome. They've flown all the way here from Colombia! And you love juggling! If you want to, stand up and clap. Or whistle. Whatever you would do to show your pleasure."

The door opened. The seven filed in. We started cheering, clapping, whistling, while they lined up before us on stage and bowed.

Carried away by Keith's instructions, we kept whooping and applauding for a while. Weirdly, the jugglers didn't look delighted but slightly annoyed.

"Oh, dear, I'm sorry," Keith said. "I've made a mistake. Forgive me. Let's try it again." And he went outside with the jugglers again, returning moments later.

"Try to forget whatever just happened. My fault. When they come in, give them the same welcome. That was good."

I was struggling to imagine what he had done wrong, but didn't have time to think it through because he called them back in. We stood, applauded, whooped and whistled as before. The jugglers lined up, bowed, looked around at us all and seemed really pleased to be there. They beamed. And the more they liked it, the longer the applause went on. They gazed around at us, as if we were old friends.

"OK," Keith said. "That's probably enough. Jugglers, you can sit down. Let me explain what just happened."

To begin, he asked the people who'd been in the audience if they noticed any difference between the first time and the second. It took us a while to think it through, but a consensus emerged: they'd looked a bit up themselves the first time, but the second time they seemed really happy.

"The first time I went out, I gave them a secret," Keith said. "I told them to be professional, but to be careful – because you're a bunch of shits." We laughed at his description of us, considered the implications of what he said, then laughed again. That was why they seemed weirdly annoyed, even hostile.

"The second time, I told them I had made a terrible mistake. They must forget what I'd said. You're not shits! This time, I told them just to look around at you all, and notice how interesting and attractive you all are. Not force it, just look around and notice."

In other words, he told them 1. to fear us, but still act professionally; 2. to adore us. At some level, unconsciously, we picked that up and applauded accordingly.

So, if speakers fear or dislike an audience, the audience will know that. And if speakers allow themselves to notice that an audience is interesting and attractive, the audience will know that.

"Remember this," Keith said, "and your audience will want to take you home."

## Leap of faith

So: I had a breakdown. And from rock bottom, I started to recover. It was slow, and I don't know that the process ever ends, but I'm alive, for which I thank the Lord every day. Here I am, writing a book that even includes the odd jokey bit. I can assure you I didn't get unwell merely because some talks went badly, so you needn't worry about that happening to you; nor because online marketers successfully filled me with a dread of penury, though it didn't help as I'd already become depressed.

Perhaps most importantly, I'm going to argue that it was substantially through talking to groups of people that I got better again.

Some of those groups were therapy groups, in which I felt safe sharing what was going on, for the simple reason that the terms of engagement were clear. It was confidential. There was no criticism of one another. We focused on ourselves. This is a very big deal: to speak in confidence takes a leap of faith, because confidentiality can't be enforced.

If this doesn't seem immediately relevant to your own situation – pish! It jolly well is. Because speaking with confidence takes a leap of faith too. You have to decide to believe that it's going to be OK delivering your talk to an industry conference, or speech at a wedding, or pitch to investors. You're in the same boat as the wrecks approaching their first group therapy session.

Happily, taking a leap of faith is salutary. To me, it was a reminder of the joy of improvisation, the joy of somehow knowing that creativity will never stop pouring into me, wherever it may come from. The joy of knowing that there's always something to say. And there really is, because if you can't think of anything else, just talk about whatever happens to be going on in the here and now. You might want to ignore it, pretend to be interested in something else, something blander, more abstract, or "more important", but that is evasion. Name the Thing!

Leaving hospital, I signed up for ongoing support from a community group run by the charity, Talk for Health. Individuals from all kinds of backgrounds joined the group to learn to speak about their experiences in something like the same safe context as therapy (or like a 12-step fellowship). There was no requirement that Talk for Health participants be mentally unwell, though I'd guess that most in my group, of approximately 25 people, were experiencing some kind of difficulty.

In one of the first sessions, we were given the opportunity to speak to the whole group for a few minutes, about anything. I leapt up to go first.

I told the group what I've told you: about admitting myself

to hospital, being put on suicide watch and so on. As I spoke, I could see that some were amazed, shocked by my candour. But to me, having talked a lot in hospital, it was easy. I didn't feel bold, or clever, or pleased with my spontaneous talk. I just knew that if I said what was truly on my mind it would give others permission to do the same. And it did.

Life is too short for the alternative, in which the first speaker tries to look good and others follow suit, and nobody learns anything.

Afterwards, in a tea break, a participant called Jo told me she was there because the company she worked for supports Talk for Health, and she wanted to see for herself how it worked. She was about my own age, smartly dressed. She said she was moved by what I'd said, and that I had an important story to tell. A story people needed to hear.

I knew she meant well. I knew that she believed what she was saying, but I wasn't ready to believe it. I was still very fragile, still regularly calling Samaritans, still believed I was totally and irredeemably useless.

But she wasn't the only person who said this kind of thing. Another was Tazeen, who I bumped into at 10 Downing Street, of all places, at a charity reception hosted by yet another journalist. Robert Peston, who was at the *Financial Times* when I was there and now has his own TV show, set up the charity Speakers for Schools to send speakers to state schools in neglected areas. Tazeen was one of their stars, and I did talks for them occasionally too.

Standing among the government ministers and celebrities, I told Tazeen what had been going on in my life recently. She laughed. But it wasn't an unkind laugh. She was just surprised to hear it inside 10 Downing Street. Then she told me she'd been through some difficulties herself – you have the advantage over me, dear reader, because, though I knew her well by that time, I had not watched her TEDx, and had no idea what she was talking about.

But I'm getting ahead of myself.

## AGM

When I was still in hospital, only days after I stopped being seen as a danger to myself, I was allowed out – believe it or not – to travel 200 miles on my own to a corporate AGM, where I was scheduled to deliver "an inspiring speech". The company in question was in communications, and I was there to help launch an initiative promoting the benefits of speaking up, and giving others a hearing.

A subject after my heart – and somewhat ironic in light of what actually happened at the AGM.

My psychiatrist looked astonished when I said I wanted to go. I was a wreck. But I had already been paid for the talk – a decent fee – and I told her that doing the talk was less scary than handing back the money.

So she let me go.

If you've not had a breakdown, you may not be aware that it feels a bit like being reborn. Doing anything afterwards, even the simplest everyday activity, can feel terrifying. Even telephoning my local pharmacy would induce panic. I felt like a beginner at everything – a beginner who just happened to have memories of doing the same kind of thing in a previous life.

So the trip itself was daunting, let alone the talk. After letting the nurses take my blood pressure and watch me taking my medication, I took a deep breath, walked out of the hospital, then towards the railway terminal. I was terrified by the simple business of collecting my pre-paid tickets; but it went OK and I realised that this too was one of those things I used to be able to do and, by some miracle, could do still.

The train journey took two hours.

Like any beginner, I prepared myself. I wrote an outline of my talk. I wrote it again, using only keywords, to drive home the structure. I drew it as a mind map, moving clockwise around the page to make the sequence obvious. Then I wrote it all out again, mumbling the words under my breath to memorise them.

Sometimes my mind drifted to difficult memories, but I disciplined myself to focus on occasions when my talks had gone well. I reminded myself that if all else failed I could just Name the Thing and free-associate. And I recited as a mantra Keith's advice about loving your audience. "Interesting and attractive... Interesting and attractive..."

At the venue, a large conference centre in a northern city, I found the woman who had engaged me to speak. I thought it was important, and only fair, to tell her that I had woken that morning in a psychiatric hospital but felt fairly sure I was going to be OK.

She took it remarkably well. In fact, she said that people close to her had been through periods of difficulty, and she had an idea of what I might be going through. Thank goodness: if something awful happened, she knew what my situation was. Mind you, I wasn't expecting anything awful.

"Interesting and attractive... Interesting and attractive..."

As the time for my talk approached, I went to the loo, as David Kendall always did – probably every speaker does. (Too much information?)

"Interesting and attractive... Interesting and attractive..."

After washing my hands, I did some stretching in front of the mirror, and again took several deep breaths, as Tazeen recommended in her TEDx, though I hadn't watched that yet. Then I walked through a corridor into the AGM, where my seat was reserved in the front row. It was a big theatre-style hall, with a steeply raked audience of hundreds of people rising high above the stage.

I had about fifteen minutes before I was on. Around this time I would usually be fitted with some kind of head microphone, or lapel mic, enabling me to walk around with my hands free, as I prefer. But this place had only handheld mics. Mine would be given to me as I walked on stage, by the person who introduced me.

I looked around. The company's board of directors sat on the raised stage behind a long table, each person seemingly absorbed in the thick pile of printed papers before them. Additionally, each one had a tabletop mic. These were turned to silent by default, but by holding down a button the speakers lit a green light and could be heard.

Speaking for myself, I would have hated to sit behind that table. As I said earlier, I don't even stand behind a podium if I can help it. It feels too "defended", like hiding in a trench in World War I, or behind a wall at the Alamo. When you're behind a wall, it's too easy to believe the people on the other side want to shoot you. Next thing you know, just to be on the safe side, you want to shoot them. Walking out to the front of the stage, hands free, undefended, feels strange and horrible the first time you do it, but I find it much more comfortable now.

All this was running through my mind – a beginner remembering things from his previous life.

I wasn't paying much attention to the ongoing Q&A session, but noticed that the atmosphere was fractious. Perhaps it was this that made me think of the black-and-white Westerns that used to be on TV all the time but have now completely disappeared. They often had a scene where the hero was in a tight spot. The baddies – Native Americans, then called Injuns, forgive me – had broken into the hero's fort. Another white man, perhaps his loveable but unheroic companion, dropped to the Injuns' feet in pitiful despair. Despising him, they finished him off. But not our hero! Oh no! Our hero, when the Injuns break into his holdout wielding tomahawks, does something startling. He rips his shirt buttons open to reveal his bare chest, as if to say: "Go ahead, drive your weapons through my heart." And the boldness of the gesture disarms them. Recognising him as a stout-hearted fellow, they let him live.

To be clear: walking to the front of the stage is not a warlike act. It's not about menacing the audience to make them put down their tomahawks. It's about feeling that you are among friends, and opening your heart.

Like I said, all this was running through my mind. I don't know where the ideas come from. They just come. You-Know-Who sends them.

The board of directors weren't opening their hearts. A microphone passed around the audience, from one investor to another. Each one had a reproachful question. The hostility was unconcealed and the board's replies were defensive. I'm not saying that to imply criticism, just to describe the tense atmosphere. Perhaps I should have expected it: this was not, after all, a children's tea party but a corporate AGM.

Even at the time, as a wreck who had come directly from a psychiatric hospital, I realised that this to-and-fro between investors and board could fit nicely into my theme of sharing what's on your mind and listening to each other. I took out my notes, skimmed through to see where I might add something. But I got distracted because the atmosphere was getting even more bad tempered. I turned around in my seat and looked at what I realised was probably the most hostile audience I'd ever faced.

I reassured myself: they were angry with the board, not with me.

"Interesting and attractive! Interesting and attractive!"

Then I caught myself. Keith never said to pretend people were interesting and attractive. He said, go on stage cheerful and just allow yourself to notice. Don't force it.

I breathed, relaxed a bit.

I was there to give the best talk I could. I was there to serve this particular audience, and the nice people who had invited me, and paid me. The audience might look hostile, but they weren't as scary as admitting myself to a psychiatric hospital. They couldn't say anything nasty about me that I hadn't already said about myself. With immense relief, I realised that I truly, profoundly wasn't afraid of them.

And then: "...welcome John-Paul Flintoff!"

Suddenly it was happening. Adrenaline kicked in, and everything slowed down. As often seems to occur, I achieved a kind of double-focus: looking out through my own eyes but also hovering above, looking down at myself like some kindly alter ego, or guardian angel. I watched John-Paul Flintoff walk to the stage, take three steps up and shake hands with the man who had introduced him, take a microphone and walk cheerfully to the front and centre. And as John-Paul Flintoff raised the mic to his mouth, somebody else's voice came through the loudspeakers.

"Our questions haven't been answered. We should cancel the speaker or have him back another day."

This was a surprise. I was in the middle of the stage, at the front, alone, holding the mic in front of hundreds of people. For a few moments, I simply couldn't fathom what was happening. Had I come on too soon? No. Was I some kind of fall guy? Maybe. Fleetingly, I wondered if the initiative I was there to help launch was really no more than a cunning device to bring an end to a difficult Q&A session. I had no idea. I looked behind me at the board members lined up behind their long table. They too seemed confused.

I looked back at the audience. A flurry of head turning led my eyes to a man sitting in the middle of a row towards the front. He had an amiable face, but looked resolute. I saw that he was holding one of the mics used for the Q&A. In a fraction of a second I concluded that it was impossible for anybody else to silence his mic while he held it, and that nobody was going to take it from him – which I wouldn't have wanted anyway.

Obviously, it's not just hostile audiences that can throw speakers off course. When Chris Toumazis and his brother scripted their sister's wedding, they came up with a joke that required a prolonged silence. But in the event their grandmother leapt into the stillness with a joke about the groom ("I fancy Theo"). "She stole our laughter," Chris told me. "We had a word with her after." But let's get back to that AGM, where I was standing at the front of the stage, staring blankly.

Other thoughts passed, uninvited but welcome, in and out of my head. The first that made itself comfortable was the delicious memory of an improvised scene I once played with my friend Jude. I remembered the appalled faces of our audience when she suddenly turned on me and I said out loud how uncomfortable this made me feel. Some had literally covered their eyes.

In no hurry, trusting in the moment, I raised my mic to my mouth. Before speaking, I looked around at everybody, taking it all in.

I didn't want to address directly the man with the mic: I didn't want to get into a debate, or make it personal. I assumed that if he felt that way, others probably felt much the same.

"Well," I said. And I paused.

"This is awkward."

Working with Jude had taught me what power can accumulate if you give enough space to the right moment.

I waited, feeling genuinely awkward but also looking down at myself and enjoying the show. "Ha! John-Paul Flintoff has really got them!" my alter ego said. "Those people can hardly bear to look!"

I had Named the Thing. Everybody knew this was awkward. They knew that I knew it was awkward. By naming it, I gave us all a chance to feast on the delicious awkwardness together. We shared an experience. We bonded.

What's more, I made time for more ideas to drift through my head. One of them came out of my mouth.

"I can see that my talk isn't wanted, not today anyway, by at least one person in the room, possibly many others too. And I don't know what to do. I don't want to get in the way. I really don't. But I would be disappointed not to do it. I have prepared, I have been paid, and I have travelled here from London. And the topic – being heard, and giving others a hearing – is very relevant. Here's what I suggest. Either I leave the stage immediately, or I give you a shorter version of what I came here to say... Perhaps you can give me a sign if you would like me to do that?"

A vigorous burst of applause. Smiles on faces.

The amiable, resolute man with the mic pressed a button to turn it off, and laid it on his lap.

And I thought: I can do this.

## Under control

I was deeply unsure whether to tell that story. For one thing: is it folly to write in a book that I have been in a psychiatric hospital (as I appear to be doing, but I haven't finished yet; maybe I'll take it out)? And another: doesn't that story about the AGM sound like the most appalling humblebrag?

Maybe, and possibly. I'll never know for sure. But

in the end I decided to tell the story because, as I said earlier, stories can be more effective than plonking down propositions and expecting people to accept them. (As ever, this applies to your talks as much as to my book.)

The proposition I want to share is hard to describe without sounding like a reversal of all I've said before about respecting your audience, being curious about your listeners' needs, wishes and fear and so on.

It might seem as if I'm suddenly proposing one of the dark manoeuvres typical of a dishonest online marketer. It's another paradox, best understood by analogy, anecdote and rhetorical elaboration.

Standing in front of those people, though in many ways a wreck, I realised that I had to exert an element of control. To assert myself, if only for as long as it would take for the audience to ask me to leave. And as you see, they quite liked my assertiveness, such as it was. I suppose it was a bit like a funambulist asking the crowd at the circus if they would like him to walk the high wire.

That's the metaphor used by Simon Callow, in his wonderful book *Being an Actor*. "Standing on the stage," he writes, "is like saying to the audience, 'look at me. Listen to me'. It says, I'm interesting, I'm talented, I'm remarkable."

Anybody who stands up in front of an audience, on a soap box, in a pulpit or on a stage, is essentially saying: "Here you are! Here's something extraordinary!"

Anyone? Really? If you aspire only to be adequate, you may have difficulty believing that you have anything extraordinary to offer. But Callow's point still applies: you must believe it's extraordinary enough to be worth saying.

And you must believe that yourself, not hope that others will believe it for you.

At no time should you be needy, Callow says, demanding anybody else's approval: "As soon as you ask the audience for approval you're done for... but you can't avoid it unless you have won your own respect. If you feel you could have done more work, your relationship to the audience will be craven, depending on their goodwill and indulgence."

When you've done enough work, you don't exercise control out of fear, but for the greater pleasure of all: Callow remembers Sir John Gielgud saying that the problem for an actor in playing *The Importance of Being Earnest* is to stop the audience from laughing at every line, so as to enable them to laugh much more every four lines.

Imagine that! Isn't it a wonderful thing to aim for: to be so good that your audience's pleasure needs to be contained.

One analogy for the control you must exert over an audience could be made with dances such as waltz, tango or jive, in which one partner leads and another follows. But this raises a difficult question: what are you leading, exactly, and how do you do it? As with dance, the answer varies. It could be that you rouse the audience to Do Something, now or later. Or you elicit audible expressions: emotional noise, like laughter or verbal utterance.

A beautiful example of both was captured by the American academic and rhetorician Garry Wills, in an article he wrote for *Esquire* magazine immediately after the assassination of Martin Luther King.

In that magazine story, Wills makes it clear that the community that mourned King had its own very particular expectations of speakers (as does any community). There, in Memphis, they drew on the traditions of Southern Baptists and the blues. Wills takes great care to spell out what that actually means: when a speaker hits a theme that moves a crowd, they cheer him on (most were men), repeating key words or answering his questions ("That's right!").

Great preachers, he says – and King was the best – can sense exactly the right time to pause or move on. Sometimes they let the crowd determine the pace, sometimes they push against it. Wills describes this kind of sermon as essentially a musical form composed of repetitions, variations and refrains.

While he was there, among the mourners, Wills watched many preachers preach. The one that really hit him was Reverend James Bevel, fourteenth and last to speak that afternoon. Wills assumed that the earlier emotional talks would have drained the grieving audience. Then he described, using direct quotes and observations in parenthesis, how Bevel built them up:

"'Dr King died on the case... You getting me?' (They're

getting him.) 'There's a false rumour going round that our leader is dead. Our leader is not dead!' ('No!' They know King's spirit lives on – half the speeches have said that already.) 'That's a false rumour.' ('Yes!' 'False!' 'Sho' nuff!' 'Tell it!') 'Martin Luther King is not –' (yes, they know, not dead; this is a form in which expectations are usually satisfied, the crowd arrives at each point with the speaker; he outruns them at peril of losing the intimate ties that slacken and go taut between each person in the room; but the real artist takes chances, creates suspense, breaks the rhythm deliberately; a snag that makes the resumed onward flow more satisfying) '– Martin Luther King is not our leader!' ('No!' The form makes them say it, but with hesitancy. They will trust him some distance; but what does he mean? The 'Sho' nuff' is not declamatory now; not fully interrogatory either; circumflexed.) 'Our leader –' ('Yes?') '– is the man –' ('What man?' 'Who?' 'Who?' Is he trying to supplant King? The trust is almost fading) '– who led Moses out of Israel.' ('Thass the man!' Resolution: all doubt dispelled; the bridge has been negotiated, left them stunned with Bevel's virtuosity.)"

## Truth has power

We're coming to the end now. It has always been my intention to write a modest book. For that reason, part of me wishes my storytelling didn't rely quite so much on stories about my own experiences, valuable though I know they might be. I only hope I have provided you with a decent balance of successes and sucksesses. (Neologism: I mean, failures.)

Anyway, I'm going to get out of the way now, and let somebody else finish. I hope that's OK.

Not long ago, my friend Brian Jenner, the speechwriter, was moved to write to parliament.

Brian believes that the ability to vocalise feelings, ideas and experiences is essential if you are to lead people, build strong relationships or maintain strong mental health. He believes that the main impediment to our greatest achievements is the fear of public speaking, the fear of appropriate self-revelation, the fear of honesty in social interactions.

So he wrote to parliament to champion oratory, to promote its value to young people – to everybody.

His submission, several pages long, is available to download from his website. But the gist of it is that teaching young people public speaking skills gives them leadership capabilities, helps them build strong relationships and maintain sound mental health.

He goes on to explain how he became a speechwriter, and talk about people who have inspired him.

He starts by describing his good fortune in being sent to the school, in Oxford, where former pupils included great exponents of expression, including William Tyndale (who first translated the Bible into English) and Sir Thomas More (England's Lord Chancellor and author of *Utopia*). At Oxford University, Brian watched leading politicians speak to the Union, as well as students who would become politicians, such as Boris Johnson. Brian lacked the confidence to speak there himself, but describes his first attempts at public speaking at Toastmasters in London. Toastmasters was established in California, during the Depression, he explains, and has since become a global movement, free to newcomers but with additional benefits to paying members.

On his first visit, Brian was invited to the podium to speak without preparation on Mars Bars. "I was paralysed with fear and had to sit down after 15 seconds." But he stuck with it, and improved.

At the speechwriters' conference Brian invited me to in Paris, several participants had, like Brian, learned to be confident speakers at Toastmasters. And like them, Brian found that his evenings at Toastmasters would qualify him as an expert on speeches. Soon, he was blessed with well-paid work writing speeches for other people.

People are often surprised to learn that speakers don't always write their own speeches, but it happens all the time. It's only a problem when the speaker hasn't had a significant part in putting the speech together or, worse, hasn't even read it before sharing it with an audience.

Today, Brian is well connected. He knows a lot of experts on speaking and rhetoric, in the UK, Europe and the US. So it's charming that, in his submission to parliament, he acknowledges how much inspiration he has drawn from people with no training at all.

In Bournemouth, where he lives, there are many recovering addicts, members of 12-step recovery programmes. Through meeting some of them, Brian became curious. Where did they get their composure?

Writing to MPs, who create government policy through their speeches and debates, Brian writes: "The 12 steps is a programme of spiritual healing, based on sharing personal accounts of recovery. It involves standing up in front of other addicts and telling stories about the insanity of your condition. The benefits accrue to the speaker, not necessarily to the listeners. Of course, nobody really wants to do this. It's incredibly stressful to say things about yourself in front of an audience. Especially if they're shameful."

For a hobby, he tells his parliamentary readers, Brian listens to 12-step shares on the internet.

"Why are they so compelling? Because to recover, you have to be honest. If you stand up and say something that's true, it has power."

# Ten steps to making the
# the very best speech you can

1. Put into a single sentence what you hope to achieve by speaking, with specifics.

2. With that outcome in mind, make notes about who your audience is, and about what they might expect of you (as opposed to somebody else).

3. Consider the location, and the timing, and how these will affect you and the audience when the time comes.

4. Think of stories that encapsulate the whole point of your talk, and the "ooh!" moments in each story that contain the key lesson, joke or revelation.

5. Make notes about how you feel about your audience, your topic, the occasion and your competence. It can be very helpful to make concrete your fears and uncertainties, rather than let them swirl around endlessly in your mind.

6. Write an outline, then fill it out and polish it up to a script.

7. Cut everything that doesn't help you to achieve your purpose. Read it aloud. Record yourself and listen back. Read it to others. Memorise the overall shape and specific phrases, if not the whole thing (preferable).

8. Get there on time.

9. Instead of focusing on yourself (am I good? am I bad?) remember at all times to be in service to your audience – notice, without forcing it, that they're interesting and attractive – even when you are there to give them a hard time, for their own good.

10. If anything "goes wrong", slow down. Trust yourself, and them. You're all in it together. And you actually do know your stuff. You're not God (or "God"), so you don't know absolutely everything. Be honest about it, and promise to follow up later.

# Q&A

*Do you have any questions?*

John-Paul Flintoff

## Question: How do you handle questions?

Answer: I announce at the beginning of a talk that I'm happy for people to raise a hand and ask questions at any time, but that they may wish to wait for the Q&A at the end. This helps people relax and keep listening, even if there's something unresolved. If possible, I add that I will also hang around for a bit afterwards in case people want to ask a question privately.

## Question: How do I deal with an online audience I can't see?

Answer: It can be easy to forget people who are watching remotely, if they're not visible. Often at the beginning I address myself to them directly, explicitly state that I'm grateful for their time and attention. I might say, "I know you may be in your pyjamas, and/or picking your nose, and that's absolutely fine; in fact I'm delighted. I just hope I will deserve your attention." Then I'll ask if there's any way they can interact with me – they may be able to turn on a camera at their end and wave, or turn on a microphone and say hi. If neither of those things are possible I might say, "Well, please just wave to the camera now, and even though I can't see you, it will be nice to imagine it." And I will say thank you, and admit that I have no idea whether they really waved, but that I like to believe they did.

### Question: How do I know what to leave out?

Answer: Think about plays and movies. When you see a character put a gun in a drawer, you know that's important. In a later scene, when the characters move towards that drawer, you have not forgotten about the gun. It raises tension. If they don't use the gun immediately, you know they will come back to it – the old chiller trick, raising tension even higher. If by the end of the movie nobody has opened the drawer and taken out the gun, you (as audience) will feel irritated and short-changed. Is the thing you want to put into your talk or presentation a gun that will never be used?

### Question: What do I do if I completely dry up?

Answer: Stop. Breathe. Take as long as you like. Contrary to what you might think, a speaker who pauses can look extremely wise, provided that his or her face isn't contorted in panic. If you find, after stopping and breathing and taking your time, that you can't think of anything more to say – say that, and enjoy the applause from an audience who will appreciate your brevity. It's possible that, while they're clapping, you might suddenly remember something important. So raise your hands to quieten them, and say it.

### Question: Is reading a speech from a script a complete no no?

Answer: In general, reading a speech is not great, but it's OK if you have to. A friend told me recently she had re-read the speech she gave at her father's funeral. "I have no idea how I managed to deliver it then as just reading it now feels extremely emotional." If you must read, look at the paper silently and look up to deliver the words with eye contact. Never speak while looking down at the paper. If you must have prompts, avoid a verbatim speech of dense type on a single page. Instead, write short notes on cue cards.

### Question: Should I direct my gaze towards a couple of people or rather try and look at everyone without really seeing them?

Answer: Spread the love (or anger, or whatever). Looking only at one or two people will freak them out and leave everybody else feeling short-changed. Look around – not generally, all over the place, which is easy to spot and looks weird. Actually look at individuals, if only fleetingly, all around the room, not just at the front. Notice that they are individuals, interesting and attractive in their own right.

### Question: Is it needy to tell your audience you don't normally make speeches, in fact you find the act terrifying?

Answer: It's a bit boring, to be honest. If you must say that, make it into a joke. Tell them you're so terrified that you might explode and express your apologies in advance for the mess.

**Question: *At a wedding, birthday or funeral, to tell the truth might be inappropriate, and actually hurt people. How much truth is too much? And is lying better?***

Answer: If you can't find anything positive to say, you're probably not the ideal speaker. Ask if somebody else can do it. If there's nobody else, and the best you can say about the deceased, or the bride, is that he or she never consumed a whole bottle of vodka before breakfast – well, say that, and apologise for having nothing more to tell. But don't lie. Never lie.

**Question: *How does speaking and presenting online change things?***

Answer: Online talks are basically the same as any other kind, but with one major difference, unknown to Cicero: your audience is simultaneously far away and up too close. It can feel overwhelmingly intimate (I've been in online talks where participants logged in from a kitchen while making breakfast and eating it, or from a bathroom while applying make-up, and even from under a duvet). And in the same event, five minutes later, you can suddenly feel like you're all on your own. The thing to remember is that your audience is probably having the same experience. So be honest – say how you are finding it. Ask people to help you out by giving real-time feedback. It doesn't have to be a survey or fancy software. Just ask questions occasionally. Because if people don't feel seen, they might quietly disappear.

# Postscript

*Often, an audience will applaud when earlier material is brought back into the story. They couldn't tell you why they applaud, but the reincorporation does give them pleasure.*

Keith Johnstone

Jo, my lawyer friend from Talk for Health continued to encourage me to tell my story, and to start by giving a talk to people in her firm. I did. Amazingly, 250 people gave up their lunchtimes to listen to me. I used slides: drawings I had made in hospital and afterwards, and was delighted to watch lawyers laugh (where that was intended) and cry at other points. I've subsequently done similar talks elsewhere. I'm still haunted by the number of young people, mostly men, whom I watched being admitted to hospital after they'd attempted suicide; and for as long as their memory is vivid, and people think my talks might help, I'll do more of them.

Jo also introduced me to Rachel Ison, the young woman who threw a fundraising birthday tea party, and who is Jo's daughter.

David Kendall has retired. He says the market for after-dinner speakers has all but dried up. He still has all the books cataloguing his talks – with dates, the stories he told, and the jokes.

Steve Chapman did a TEDx talk wearing a mask, in the persona of his own inner critic. It was brilliant, and went viral. Check it out.

Patrick Kinna died in 2009, aged 95.

Tazeen Ahmad died in 2019, aged 48, leaving two sons and many friends. You can watch her TEDx online. Take a look. Leave a comment.

# Further reading

*A History of Reading*, Alberto Manguel (Flamingo)

*Bech*, John Updike (Penguin)

*Being an Actor*, Simon Callow (Penguin)

*By Heart*, Ted Hughes (Faber & Faber)

*Blood, Toil, Tears and Sweat : The Speeches of Winston Churchill*, David Cannadine (Penguin)

*Collins English Thesaurus* (Collins)

*Complete Works*, William Shakespeare (Oxford)

*Daring Greatly*, Brené Brown (Penguin)

*Dr Johnson* (Oxford anthology)

*Elements of Eloquence*, Mark Forsyth (Icon)

*Exercises in Style*, Raymond Queneau (Alma Classics)

*Explosive Preaching*, Ron Boyd-MacMillan (Paternoster)

*First You Write a Sentence*, Joe Moran (Penguin)

*Gwynne's Grammar*, N M Gwynne (Ebury)

*How Plays Work*, David Edgar (Nick Hern Books)

*How to Pray*, Pete Greig (Hodder & Stoughton)

*Impro*, Keith Johnstone (Methuen)

*Influence*, Robert Cialdini (Harper Business)

*King James Bible* (Oxford)

*Lend Me Your Ears*, Max Atkinson (Vermilion)

*Macaulay's Essays* (Longman)

*Ogilvy on Advertising*, David Ogilvy (Welbeck)

*On Speaking Well*, Peggy Noonan (HarperCollins)

*Oxford Book of Aphorisms* (Oxford)

*Oxford Dictionary of Quotations* (Oxford)

# Further Reading

*Penguin Book of Historical Speeches*, Brian MacArthur
  (Penguin)
*Penguin Book of Modern Speeches*, Brian MacArthur
  (Penguin)
*Pictures on a Page*, Harold Evans (Pimlico)
*Poems by Adrian Mitchell* (Bloodaxe)
*Poems of Lord Byron* (Oxford)
*Roget's Thesaurus* (Penguin)
*Selected Essays*, William Hazlitt (Penguin)
*Selected Prose*, John Donne (Penguin)
*40 Sonnets*, Don Paterson (Faber & Faber)
*Stick It Up Your Punter*, Chris Horrie and Peter Chippindale
  (Pocket Books)
*Thank You for Arguing*, Jay Heinrichs (Penguin)
*The Art of Speeches and Presentations*, Philip Collins (Wiley)
*The King's English*, Kingsley Amis (Penguin)
*The Language Instinct*, Steven Pinker (Penguin)
*The Madness of Crowds*, Douglas Murray (Bloomsbury
  Continuum)
*The New Journalism*, Tom Wolfe (Picador)
*The Poet's Manual and Rhyming Dictionary*, Frances Stillman
  (Thames & Hudson)
*The Righteous Mind*, Jonathan Haidt (Penguin)
*The Simple Subs Book*, Leslie Sellers (Pergamon)
*Theatre of the Oppressed*, Augusto Boal (Pluto Press)
*The Visual Display of Quantitative Information*, Edward Tufte
*Vital Speeches of the Day*, David Murray (ed)
*When They Go Low...*, Philip Collins (Fourth Estate)
*Words and Pictures*, Quentin Blake (Tate)
*You Talkin' To Me*, Sam Leith (Profile)

# Acknowledgements

For supporting me in body, mind and spirit, for seeing a friend in a stranger (and promise in an idea), for publishing this, for feeding me, cheering me up, and on, holding the fort, giving us a beautiful home to stay in several summers in a row, providing accounting services, giving me another nephew, turning up unexpectedly inside 10 Downing Street, walking beside me with Eeyore strapped to your bike, giving me lunch, praying for me, preaching with God in your mouth, becoming violent towards me in an impro routine, inviting me to meet fellow speechwriters in Paris and Cambridge, getting me involved at The School of Life, on stage in Athens, on stage at that AGM, and inside your law firm, sharing your own experience of speaking for the first time, creating Talk for Health and having me be part of it, sending me cartoons in the post, trusting me to do things at Wigtown, idling in the pub near the old Academy, inviting me to Belfast, for accessing my creative conscience, for five one-day MBAs, for conversations off Sloane Square, trusting me to write about Brendan Barns years ago, putting me on that soapbox, and thrusting me upon David Kendall, for inviting me to Devon so that I would go in subsequent years to Yorkshire and Shropshire, for agreeing to read this in manuscript, and for sharing your stories as well as listening to mine, thank you to Harriet Green, Nancy Flintoff, Jaime Marshall, Aurea Carpenter, Rebecca Nicolson, Ian and Deirdre Flintoff, Martin Brooke, Steve Iley, Karen Dobres,

# Acknowledgements

Ben Akers, Jack and Sue Green, Alice Jolly, Bankim Thanki, Chris Kay, Tom Bryant, Crispin Flintoff, Tazeen Ahmad, Mark Lebon, Philippa Perry, Will Lewis, Ayla Lepine, Jeremy Fletcher, Jan Rushton, Steve Chapman, Jude Claybourne, Brian Jenner, Morgwn Rimel and Caroline Brimmer, Marie Efpraxiadis, Jacci Marcus, Jo Gubbay and Gabriella Wickes, Rachel Ison, Nicky Forsythe, Robert Twigger, Adrian Turpin, Tom Hodgkinson, Eva Grosman, Chrissy Levett, Kirsty Buck, Angela Mooney, Michael Watts, Cathy Galvin, Mark Edmunds, Mary Morris, Andrew Morris, Deb Shedden, Claire Murray, Barbara Fashola, Rosie Simpson, Laura Cameron, Felice Hardy, Lynda Thompson, Rachel Krish, Viv Bennett, Kristel Tonstad, Laura Tan, and fellow patients, therapists and staff at the Nightingale.

Not necessarily in that order. You know what you did.

To people I have forgotten to name: I'm grateful for your kindness, beg forgiveness for my faulty memory and hope I did at least say thank you at the time.

# About the Author

John-Paul Flintoff is a journalist, artist and performer who has delivered talks across four continents to audiences of as many as 5,000 people. He has worked as a writer and editor at the *Financial Times* and *The Sunday Times*, trained in improvisational theatre and has published five books, including *How to Change the World*. He lives in London.